# Prayer

# A Practical Guide

## Martin Pable, OFM Cap.

## Foreword by Alice Camille

**ACTA**

ASSISTING CHRISTIANS TO ACT

PUBLICATIONS

***Prayer: An Introduction***
by Martin Pable, OFM Cap.

Foreword by Alice Camille
Edited by Gregory F. Augustine Pierce
Cover design by Tom A. Wright
Typesetting by Desktop Edit Shop, Inc.

Scripture quotations are from the *New Revised Standard Version of the Bible,* copyright © 1989 by the Division of Christian Education of the National Council of the Churches of Christ in the U.S.A. Used with permission. All rights reserved.

Published by:   ACTA Publications
Assisting Christians To Act
4848 N. Clark Street
Chicago, IL 60640-4711
773-271-1030
actapublications@aol.com

Library of Congress Catalog Number: 2002092798

ISBN: 0-87946-235-3

Printed in the United States of America

Year: 08 07 06 05 04 03 02
Printing: 10 9 8 7 6 5 4 3 2 1

# Contents

# Foreword

**by Alice Camille**
**author of *Invitation to Catholicism***

Many of us have looked for a great little book on prayer and found resources that were neither little nor great. If you are not naturally transported into rapt contact with the divine at the mere lighting of a candle or haven't already got your particular "spirituality" all figured out, then these kinds of guides may not be all that helpful. Before you forfeit the privilege of praying altogether, however, spend a little time with Father Martin Pable on the following pages. His is a simple and comforting introduction to the business of prayer that has the ring of authenticity to it. No rabbits come out of hats here, no mystical smoke-and-mirrors will confuse you, and no previous heavenly visions are required! This is a book by a man who prays, speaking to others who do—or who sure would like to. It's a perfect guide for those just coming to understand the Catholic approach to prayer, as well as a clarifying affirmation for those who have been at the task of praying all along.

If you've already got a shelf full of primers on prayer at home, you know that books on the subject often seem written for mystics-in-training rather than for people who have jobs, families and community responsibilities. For those of us who feel hopelessly trapped in the three-dimensional world of five senses, prayer is a rarified experience for which we hardly seem to qualify. Happily, Father Pable keeps prayer close to home and to ordinary life. He takes the root experiences of the prayer lives of Catholics—traditional prayers we already know, the handiness of scripture, the pleasure of quiet and the ease of natural conversation, even the celebration of the Mass—and shows us how to use these simple tools to establish an enlivening relationship with God. He builds the case for thinking about prayer as a means to that vital relationship and not as a way of arm-wrestling God into taking our side or sharing our concerns. God already shares our concerns, he argues, and God already wants for us greater blessings than we even know to ask for.

If you've ever wondered if praying is worthwhile, if asking for healing or a blessing is cheating "God's will," or what it means when your prayers are not met with the results you hoped for, you'll find some thoughtful reflections on these and other matters here. You'll also find a variety of approaches to the business of prayer that are straightforward and straight from the heart. If you try them all, like Goldilocks in the fairy tale, sooner or later you'll come upon one that is "just right" for you. As Father Pable reminds us, the Holy Spirit longs to be expressed through us as much as we hunger to give voice to our prayer. If the desire for prayer goes both ways, how can we lose?

*Prayer: A Practical Guide* is the first title in a series of short, conversational and informative books about the Catholic life of faith. Each one is designed to be useful for both the individual seeker as well as for parish groups and schools. Each book includes questions for reflection and a suggested faith response. The series was inspired by the response to the book *Invitation to Catholicism,* which I wrote as a glimpse into the Catholic world-view for newcomers, outsiders, old seekers and anyone interest-ed in what it means to be Catholic. The new series emerging from that book shares the same perspective. Through this series, we hope to spread the invitation to Catholicism even more widely, offering focused attention on individual aspects of faith-filled living.

Christianity is a passionate vocation for those who embrace it fully. And the Catholic tradition holds the richness of many generations, tested teaching, a worldwide community, and a sacramental order of worship that could be mined for a lifetime without exhausting its meaning. If you've been looking for a great little book on prayer, you've come to the right place.

## Chapter One

# Why Pray?

*Prayer.* The very sound of the word in English is beautiful. It arouses feelings of peacefulness, of reverence, of the presence of the transcendent, the sacred, the holy, the divine. Even if we no longer attend church, we are drawn to prayer. We want to pray. We know it is good to pray. Our only question is *how* to pray, which will be the focus of this book.

But first we need to ask an important preliminary question: *Why* do we pray? My short answer is that we *need* to pray. We human beings are "hard wired" for prayer. We experience ourselves as finite, fragile and vulnerable creatures who do not have full control over our own existence, much less over the universe. The terrorist attacks throughout the world have brought this truth home to us in unmistakable terms. When such events occur, we pray individually or with our families or gather in groups to pray—for the victims and their families, for the rescue workers, for our leaders, and indeed for ourselves. We know we are dealing with something far beyond our comprehension or control. It is the same sense of neediness and human limitation that prompted Abraham Lincoln, despite all the powers of the American presidency, to confess: "I have been driven to my knees very often by the sheer realization that I had nowhere else to go."

### Prayer as a Human Hunger

Beyond our basic need in times of trouble, there is another, inner dynamic or energy that keeps moving us toward prayer. It is what spiritual writers call "our hunger for God." A little reflection on our own experience will verify this. For no matter how many possessions we acquire, or successes we attain, or pleasures we taste, or friendships we cherish—we are never quite satisfied. There is always something more that we crave, something that will totally fill up that hole of emptiness we feel

**7**

in the center of our very souls. In our silent, honest moments—especially in that sense of letdown we feel after we experience even the most delightful time—the thought slides into our minds: This was wonderful, but it is not enough. We somehow sense that we are made for the infinite and eternal.

It was the same profound feeling that drove Saint Augustine to utter those memorable words: "Thou hast made us for thyself, O Lord; and our hearts will be restless till they rest in Thee!" Centuries earlier the Psalmist, knowing the same spiritual hunger, had cried out: "As the deer longs for flowing streams, so my soul longs for you, O God. My soul thirsts for God, for the living God" (Psalm 42:1-2). Indeed, we do not live by bread alone, or by exciting experiences alone, or by worldly fame and glory alone. Our souls desire nothing less than a personal relationship with God. That is the powerful force drawing us to prayer.

### Prayer as Building Relationship

Our desire for relationship with God is matched (or, even better, outstripped) by God's desire to connect with us. Why should God want that? I have no idea. Even the Psalmist wondered why God should be mindful of us poor mortals, or care about our fate (see Psalm 8:5). God surely does not need us for completion or perfection. God is fullness of life and perfection. But, as the Bible states so boldly, the very nature of God is to love (see 1 John 4:16). And the very nature of love is to share itself, to pour itself out, to seek relationship. When love gives itself, it generates hope and goodness and life in others.

The Bible further reveals that our God is "for us," not against us (see Romans 8:31). God does not sit in splendid isolation in the heavens beyond. No, the God of the Bible is One who is deeply, passionately involved in our human lives.

But if God desires relationship with us, it is not to enrich or enhance the divine being. Rather, it is to bless and enliven *us*. Which brings us to the purpose of prayer. We too easily imagine prayer as asking for things we need or desire. And that indeed is one form of prayer—the prayer of petition, which we will discuss in a later chapter. However, the point I wish to stress

**8**

now is that the primary purpose of all prayer is *to grow in our relationship with God.*

## A Definition of Prayer

It may help at this point to share with you my own definition of prayer: Prayer is any act whereby we consciously attend to the presence of God within us or around us. Let me comment on this definition.

First, note the word *any.* Prayer is not limited to reciting words, whether our own or someone else's. That is certainly one form of prayer, but there are many others. We can sing a song or listen to prayerful music. We can quietly reflect on some word or truth that just struck us in a new way. We can gaze lovingly at a sleeping child. We can simply remain in silent wonder at the mystery that surrounds us. All are forms of prayer.

Second, the focus of prayer is *the presence of God.* We saw earlier the great truth that God is continually inviting us into relationship. That is what makes prayer possible: The first movement comes from God, not from us.

But third, prayer happens only when we *consciously attend* to God's presence. Paying attention is our response to God's gracious initiative. By doing so, we complete the circle.

And finally, our awareness of God's presence may come either from *within us* (our anxiety about a loved one, our need for comfort in a loss, our gratitude for a favor received); or it may arise from something *around us* or *outside ourselves* (hearing beautiful music, beholding a glorious nature scene, receiving a letter or call from a good friend, reading or hearing a particularly pertinent homily or message from the Bible).

It is not difficult to see, then, that prayer is simply *a form of communication.* What makes it unique is that the "other person" in the dialogue is God.

## The Nature of Human Relationships

If the purpose of prayer is to grow in our relationship with God, then it would help to draw some insights from the way human relationships grow. If you have ever been married or had a good friendship, you know a great deal about this.

For one thing, people grow in their relationship by spending time with one another. It is just not possible to maintain a friendship without doing this. Which is precisely why some relationships fail. Note the word *spend*. Some people are simply not willing to pay the price of spending time to nurture the relationship. They are too preoccupied with other goals and pursuits, and the friendship dies for lack of feeding. It is the same with our relationship with God. We may rhapsodize about our profound longing to know and love God. But if we're not willing to spend time in prayer, in the presence of God, our relationship remains at a superficial level.

What else do friends do? They grow in knowledge of each other. "Getting to know you" is one of the joys of a relationship. This is a two-fold process. First, I have to be willing to reveal myself to you, to let you get to know me. This requires a certain level of self-disclosure. I need to let you in, at some level, to my private world. Not just where I was born and went to school, or what jobs I've had, or my favorite sports or movies. But deeper: What brings me joy, deep-down satisfaction? What am I afraid of? What are my hopes and dreams? What are some of my wounds from the hurts of life? What are my strongest beliefs and values? Who is God for me?

Likewise, I will be willing to get to know you—not just superficially but at that deeper level of heart and soul. That will take time and effort, and it will be risky. After all, if I let you know who I really am, you may get scared and run away—even reject me. And if I get to know you too well, I may do the same. This, it seems to me, is why many marriages fail. The couple did not spend the time and effort to really come to know each other. They kept their knowledge at the superficial level ("She's so pretty and outgoing;" "He's such a fun-loving guy"). But after the marriage, the deep-seated differences become painfully evident, and the couple walk away in disillusionment. Or they stay together, but the cry can be heard by anyone who's listening: "We don't communicate. There's no real sharing."

There is one more way that human relationships grow. That is, people start to care about one another. One's joys, fears, hopes and dreams become as important as the other's. If we are friends, I want you to succeed. Even more, I want you to love and accept yourself, even if you don't succeed. I care about your ailing parents, I hurt with you when your workplace is demeaning, and so forth. That is the nature of the best of human relationships.

### The Nature of Our Relationship with God

Our relationship with God grows in similar ways. And the catalyst for that growth is prayer—communication, spending time with God, caring about what God cares about. So we need to make the effort, in prayer, to share with God our honest concerns and needs, our worries and our hopes and our struggles. Doesn't God already know these things? Surely. But in the very act of talking with God about them, we are naming them more clearly for ourselves.

Moreover, in prayer we can ask to see our life more truly, in the light of God's transcendent view of it. At the same time, we can come to know God more clearly, because prayer purifies our false and inadequate images of the divine. We pray to know the true God as revealed in scripture and by the collective wisdom of the church. "Getting to know you" is as necessary in our relationship with God as with any other person.

And lastly, in prayer we come to care more deeply about what God cares about. We begin to see, for example, that God doesn't much care who wins the World Series or the Academy Awards, or whether we are getting bald, or even that other people recognize our achievements. We learn that God does care about justice for all people, especially the poor, the unborn and the elderly. We come to understand that God wants us to love our neighbors, even those who don't love us, and to act in accord with Christ's teachings, even if we are criticized for it.

### Resistance to Prayer

Prayer is the privileged means for humans to grow in relationship with God. We've seen that prayer can take many forms, and each of us will find ways that best suit our temperament. Now, here is an interesting question: If prayer is such a normal, natural response to God's gracious action in our lives, why do

**11**

we tend to resist it, not take time for it, find excuses to avoid it? I have a hunch that it is because of fear. Could it be that we are, at some level, afraid to develop a real relationship with God?

All relationships involve risk. If we really open up, reveal our inmost thoughts and feelings, remove the masks that hide us—will God reject us? Or if we begin to understand the things God cares about—will we have to change our priorities? Will God ask something of us that we are not prepared to do?

And yet something deep inside us wants this kind of relationship with God. We want Someone whom we can approach just as we are, without playing any games. We want Someone who will accept us with all our imperfections but also challenge us to become our best self (without demanding more of us than we are capable of at the moment). Scripture assures us that this is precisely the kind of relationship God offers us.

As a matter of fact, Christians of all ages have discovered a wondrous truth: When we deepen our relationship with God we find in ourselves strengths and capacities we never knew we had—including the capacity to endure pain and hardship. This is simply the fruit of love. It was this love that prompted Clare of Assisi to exclaim, "Once I came to know the grace of my Lord Jesus Christ, no pain has been bothersome, no penance too severe, no weakness too hard to bear."

### Progressing in Prayer

People sometimes feel discouraged at their seeming lack of "progress" in prayer. Please do not worry about this. Progress in prayer is difficult to measure. What is the proper standard or measuring stick? If you are making sincere efforts, day after day, to place yourself in the holy presence of God, or to read God's word in scripture, or to speak to God about what is in your heart—you are praying. You may not feel enraptured or greatly comforted. But, as Jesus said to Martha: "There is need of only one thing" (Luke 10:42). If we pray, no matter how poorly we think we are doing, we are growing in our relationship with God.

The little parable Jesus told about the growth of the kingdom of God can easily be applied to our life of prayer. The seed grows "of its own accord," without the farmer knowing how (see Mark 4:26-29). So it is with prayer. If we but "pay attention" to the presence of God through prayer, God communicates divine life to us, even if we do not know exactly how this happens.

### Questions for Reflection and Discussion

1. Name three times or situations that drive you to pray.

2. What is your own definition of prayer?

3. What do you find most difficult about prayer? Where does your resistance to prayer come from?

4. What do you think of the idea of prayer as primarily a means of building a relationship with God? How is your relationship with God like your relationship with your friends and loved ones? How is it different?

5. What do you do when you feel discouraged in prayer? What are the ways that you get back on track in your prayer life?

---

### Prayer Activity

Write a letter or a poem to God, describing your hunger for the holy, the sacred, the eternal, the transcendent, the ultimately meaningful in your life. Consider sharing your letter or poem with a family member, a close friend, or a priest or minister.

---

## Chapter Two

# Praying Traditional Prayers

Most of us Catholics grew up learning certain "formula" prayers from our parents or teachers. We memorized, for example, the Sign of the Cross, the Our Father, the Hail Mary, prayers before and after meals, perhaps the Act of Contrition. These are prayers that someone else has composed and handed on to us. We treasure them because they remind us of the great truths of our faith. They put us in touch with mysteries that are beyond our immediate experience. Some, like the Our Father and the Hail Mary, are based on the words of scripture. And once we learn them it is easy to pray them any time or place. Personally, I spontaneously find myself praying Hail Marys when I'm driving through a thunderstorm or a snowstorm. I'm not able to pay attention to the words because I'm concentrating on the road. But I know what I'm doing: I'm asking my heavenly Mother to intercede with God to help me get through safely.

But this points out the limitation of formula prayers: It is easy to slip into just saying words without really praying. Our mind can float almost anywhere while we are reciting the formula. Still, such prayers are valuable. Recall the definition of prayer I offered in the previous chapter: any act whereby we consciously attend to the presence of God within us or around us. In formula prayer, even when we are distracted, we are at least *trying* to pay attention to the presence of God. We are giving expression to our desire to grow in our relationship with the divine. Many people have told me about their habit of praying while driving to and from their jobs. It is often a combination of formula prayer and spontaneous prayers of gratitude and intercession. But it is usually accompanied by distractions.

Let's talk a bit about distractions in prayer. Certainly we should try to avoid them or banish them when they emerge.

But with the exception of those who have the gift of mystical prayer, I don't think it's possible for us to avoid all distractions in prayer. And I believe God understands that our human minds are not entirely disciplined.

Somewhere I read or heard a story about Saint Francis de Sales, that wonderful teacher of prayer. In one of his sermons he mentioned that it is practically impossible for humans to pray without any distractions. Afterwards a man approached him and claimed that he could do so. The good bishop was impressed, but he decided to put the man to the test. "If you can pray the entire Our Father without distractions," the saint said, "I'll give you my horse." The man began eagerly, "Our Father, who art in heaven, hallowed be thy name; thy kingdom come..." Suddenly he stopped and said to the bishop, "Do I get the saddle too?" You can almost hear the smiling saint: "I rest my case!"

My point is that it is not our success but our sincere effort in prayer that is pleasing to God.

### A Meditation on The Lord's Prayer

Sometimes our recitation of a formula prayer can be deepened by praying it slowly and reflectively, turning the words or phrases over in our mind to probe their deeper spiritual meaning. Here is an example of how we might do this with the Lord's Prayer:

*"Our Father"*
I know, Lord, that you are neither male nor female, that our gender words do not adequately express your divine nature. Your Son Jesus taught us to address you as Father because that is how he experienced you. For myself, sometimes I perceive you as a strong, loving father who keeps challenging me to be my best self, yet patient and gentle with my weaknesses. Other times I experience you as a tender mother who is there to comfort me when I'm hurting or troubled. But you are not only *my* father/mother; you are *our* Divine Parent. I belong to a wonderful family, a global commu-

nity of sisters and brothers who acknowledge you as the origin, the nurturer, and the final end of our human existence. How good it is to know that "You have made them"—and me—"a little lower than God, and crowned them with glory and honor" (Psalm 8:5).

### "Who art in heaven"

This phrase reminds me, my God, that you are not only close to me but also far beyond me. Even though, as the Psalmist said, I am only "a little lower" than you, nevertheless I will never be your equal. You are Creator, I am creature. This is a good and holy truth. It is a bulwark against any tendency I may have toward pride or arrogance. Sometimes I am tempted to "play God," to imagine that I am somehow more than human, that I can control my life very well by myself. What nonsense. The truth is, I need you, my God. Every breath I take is your gift to me. There is a wondrous mystery here: You are both my Parent, loving and close to me, and also my awesome God, before whom I bow in adoration. Help me always to hold these two truths in balance.

### "Hallowed be thy name"

To me this means, "May we reverence the holiness of your name." It strikes me that words like reverence and holiness are hardly ever heard nowadays. Our culture thinks it is "cool" to be irreverent. And holiness is equated with "goody two-shoes"—the ultimate put-down. We (and I include myself) invoke your name in exclamations and curses as often as in prayer. So this phrase calls me to hold your name sacred, both in my speech and in my heart. Moreover, since a person's name in Jewish culture was synonymous with the person, I want to honor *you*. And I pray that everyone in the world will do the same, not only in speech but also in action. This means offering you prayerful worship and caring for the people you have created in your image.

**17**

*"Thy kingdom come...on earth as it is in heaven"*
Lord, I don't think you care about having possession
of a geographic kingdom. So "kingdom" here must be
more about your reign, your vision, your direction for
our world. Your dream, so to speak, is that gradually
every person and nation will come to acknowledge
love as the sovereign ruler over the whole universe.
Your kingdom coming would mean that the fullness
of your peace and love is spilling over into the entire
world, putting an end to all divisions and uniting all
people together as sisters and brothers. I once attended a retreat given by my Capuchin brother, Michael
Crosby, where he talked about "praying the Our
Father as a subversive act." He noted that when the
early Christians offered this prayer they were implicitly undermining the Roman social order. They were
saying, "May God's kingdom rule the world, not the
Roman Empire. May God's name, not Caesar's, be
honored as divine. May God's will, not the emperor's,
be fulfilled everywhere." I was moved by Crosby's
insight, and I saw the connection with our own time
and culture. Yes, Lord, may your kingdom come—on
earth as it is in heaven. And may you grant me the
knowledge and strength I need to help bring that
about.

*"Thy will be done on earth as it is in heaven"*
My God, you know how fiercely I cling to my personal freedom, my own will. It is said that the angels in
heaven are swift to carry out your will in all things. It
is not always that way here on earth. Sometimes,
when I am fervent in prayer, I may say something like,
"Lord, I surrender my will entirely to you. Help me to
desire and to fulfill your holy will in all things." And I
believe I really mean it. But before the day is over I am
likely to say (in deed if not in word): "...in all things
except this one." My fervor for you and my self-will
are on a collision course. I know that Jesus said clear-

ly: "If you love me, you will keep my commandments" (John 14:15). And John the disciple wrote, "Let us love, not in word or speech, but in truth and action" (1 John 3:18). I know it is all too easy to speak words of love, but the real test of love is in my actions, my decisions. My God, I am grateful for the many free choices you allow me each day. But when there is a clash between your will and my own, please help me to embrace yours, whatever the cost—and to do it joyfully.

*"Give us this day our daily bread"*
I notice how the first half of the prayer is centered on you, my God—your name, your kingdom, your will. Only now do we focus on our own needs. The first is so simple: "our daily bread." Unlike vast numbers of people in the world, I don't have to worry about basic necessities: food and water, clothing, decent housing, health care. I feel ashamed when I realize how often I take all these for granted instead of being profoundly grateful. But does "our daily bread" include other needs as well? I believe it does. I need love and acceptance from other persons. I need encouragement when I'm going through a difficult time. I need good health and energy to continue my work. Sometimes I need correction because I am drifting off the spiritual course. So when I pray "Give us this day our daily bread," I am asking you, my God, for everything I need to live as your beloved child. I hope I am not asking for things that are merely my selfish wants rather than genuine needs. And when I say "this day," I am asking for the grace to live in the present moment. I am all too prone to project into the future, to be agitated about what I may have to face down the road. Help me to live as your Son Jesus directed us: "Do not worry about tomorrow" (Matthew 6:34).

*"And forgive us our trespasses as we forgive those who trespass against us"*

Here we are accepting a basic truth of our humanity: We are sinners and in need of forgiveness. My Lord, how comforting it is to know that you do not reject us when we mess up. As long as we admit our sin, repent of it, and turn back to you, you are always there to meet us with divine mercy. But then you expect us to extend forgiveness to those who may have hurt or offended us. That's the hard part. It's so much easier to "make them pay," to maintain the stony silence, to hold the grudge. It seems you are asking us to go against our human nature. In reality, though, you are simply asking us to be true to our deeper, spiritual nature. For we are, after all, created in your image. If you are so willing to forgive us, how can we be unwilling to forgive one another? In any case, what is the alternative—to hold on to our anger, to nurse our injury, to perpetuate the negative energy? Is that what I want? No, Lord. I want to fashion myself in your image. I really believe that there are few things more beautiful than when human beings ask or grant forgiveness to one another. Help me, my God, to live out this part of the Lord's Prayer—especially when I would rather not.

*"And lead us not into temptation"*

These words are better understood when they are translated differently: "And do not bring us to the time of trial" (New Revised Standard) or "And do not put us to the test" (New Jerusalem Bible). The idea, Lord, is that we are still spiritually fragile. If our virtue is tested too severely, we might not stand firm; we may fail the test. The trial or test might be a temptation to sin. But it may also be the loss of a job, the rebellion of a child, a broken marriage, a serious illness, the death of a loved one—whatever might strain our capacity to endure. We do not pray to be spared from all trials, because then we might never mature spiritually. But we pray, Lord, that you will be with us in our time of testing, that you will provide us with the strength and the will to come through the trial with dignity and without losing our confidence in you.

*"But deliver us from evil"*
Most translations render this: "And deliver us from the evil one" (i.e., Satan). Yes, my God, the worst thing that could happen to me is to fall from your grace and to take the path of sin. I have seen it happen to others, and I know well that it is not beyond me. Saint Paul has warned us, "If you think you are standing, watch out that you do not fall" (1 Corinthians 10:12). So I ask you, Lord, as I conclude the prayer, to watch over all of us and keep us from all that would lead us away from you.

The above meditation is but one example of how a familiar prayer can take on richer meaning if we spend time reflecting upon the words. A similar process can be used with any of our formula prayers. At different times or circumstances of our life, such a meditation will yield different understandings and insights. Our prayer life is never static. Like the rest of our life, it grows and develops—provided we are paying attention to the God who calls us into relationship.

### Praying the Rosary
Another traditional formula prayer with which most Catholics are familiar is the rosary. During the Second World War my family would gather every night after supper to pray the rosary for peace. I had three older sisters and a younger brother. None of us were particularly enthused about this nightly ritual. It was just part of our daily routine. But somehow it felt good to know that we were praying for peace and were connected to many other families who were doing the same thing at roughly the same time. Years later, after my ordination, I stopped praying the rosary. I'm not sure why, except that it didn't seem to nour-

ish my spiritual life. But later I went back to it. I did so for two reasons: one, every time the Virgin Mary appears on earth, she asks us to pray the rosary for peace and for the conversion of the world; and two, I just felt I was missing a valuable form of prayer.

It strikes me as ironic that as our culture becomes more secularized and many people no longer pray the rosary, there is an increase in the use and display of beads in other contexts. They are hanging on walls, around people's necks, from the rearview mirrors of cars. What is their fascination? I don't know for sure, but I suspect that beads symbolize some deep-lying religious sensibility, something to cling to in our moments of heightened anxiety or vulnerability.

And how are we to explain the current popularity of meditation practices—many of them from the East or from primitive cultures—that feature the use of repetitive words or phrases (often called mantras)? In many ways, this chanting sounds a lot like the Catholic rosary. It seems that many cultures have discovered that repetitive prayer can have the effect of gently linking us to the love at the heart of the universe.

The rosary emerged at a time in Christian history when masses of people were illiterate. Often they had lost touch with the great stories of Christ's incarnation, suffering and death, resurrection and ascension, and with the central role of Mary in all those events. When Christians were taught how to pray the rosary, they were urged to recite the simple formula prayers while reflecting on fifteen of those biblical stories. It was a wonderful catechetical tool, similar to the stained-glass windows in the great cathedrals that depicted the truths of faith in visual images.

One advantage of the rosary as a form of prayer is that it does not require a high degree of concentration. We can pray it in the quiet of our room; but we can also do so while walking or driving or waiting in the doctor's office. But if it is going to be more than rote recitation, we need some familiarity with the various mysteries (Joyful, Sorrowful, Glorious) that the rosary recalls. Some years ago a very helpful form of praying the rosary was developed: the so-called "scriptural rosary." It is prayed in the standard way, except that a different line from scripture pertaining to the mystery for that decade is inserted between each Hail Mary. This practice serves to help us keep our mind focused on the mystery. The disadvantage of this method is that you need to have a booklet listing the Bible verses handy while you are praying the beads. For myself, I simply try to focus on a single line from scripture for each different decade.

The rosary is a tried and traditional form of prayer; but it is certainly not obligatory for all Catholics. We are free to use or not use it, or to use it occasionally, or to use it at various times in our life. Like all prayer, it is helpful if it brings us into relationship with God, and it is not helpful if it does not.

## Praying the Psalms

One final type of formula prayer I would like to suggest is praying the Psalms. I don't think we Catholics realize how deeply the Psalms are woven into our prayer life, especially our liturgical prayer. At every Mass we pray a psalm response after the first reading, and many of our hymns are based on lines from the Psalms.

It is good for us to remember that these prayers were not composed by philosophers or theologians speculating on the meaning of life. They came forth from the hearts of the people and their direct experience of life. The ancient Hebrews experienced blessing and healing and did what came naturally to them—they praised God in prayer. They were in need or in danger and cried to God for help. They were hurt by life's misfortunes and inequities and voiced their complaints to God. As time went on, these prayers were memorized by the community and many were set to music, taking the form of poetic songs.

What I love about the Psalms is that they are so honest. The Hebrew people felt free enough with God to be completely honest. They could shout for joy, lament with tears, agonize with doubt, argue with God, all with no fear of reprisals. They could do that because they really believed that prayer is communication, a way of deepening our relationship with God. Let us look at a few examples.

23

## Psalms of Thanksgiving

Here are two examples of this genre. The first is the prayer of one who has experienced God's healing in time of sickness:

> I will extol you, O Lord, for you have drawn me
>    up...
> O Lord my God, I cried to you for help, and you
>    have healed me...
> You have turned my mourning into dancing;
> You have taken off my sackcloth and clothed me
>    with joy,
> So that my soul may praise you and not be silent.
> O Lord my God, I will give thanks to you forever.
>                          —Psalm 30:1-2, 11-12

The second is a more general psalm of thanksgiving for receiving help in time of need:

> I give you thanks, O Lord, with my whole heart...
> I bow down toward your holy temple and give
>    thanks to your name,
>    for your steadfast love and your faithfulness;
> for you have exalted your name and your word
>    above everything.
> On the day I called, you answered me,
> you increased my strength of soul...
> Though I walk in the midst of trouble...
> you stretch out your hand, and your right hand
>    delivers me.
> The Lord will fulfill his purpose for me;
> your steadfast love, O Lord, endures forever.
> Do not forsake the work of your hands.
>                          —Psalm 138:1-3, 7-8

Clearly, these psalms express a deep sense of gratitude to God for blessings or favors actually experienced by the composers. At those times in our own lives when we cannot find words equal to the gratefulness in our hearts, we may turn to one of these praise or thanksgiving psalms from the Bible.

## A Psalm of Petition

In this psalm the author is in some kind of stressful situation and is convinced that only God can bring help and deliverance:

> In you, O Lord, I seek refuge; do not let me ever
> be put to shame;
> in your righteousness deliver me.
> Incline your ear to me, rescue me speedily.
> Be a rock of refuge for me, a strong fortress to
> save me...
> Be gracious to me, O Lord, for I am in distress;
> my eye wastes away from grief, my soul and body
> also.
> For my life is spent with sorrow, and my years
> with sighing;
> my strength fails because of my misery, and my
> bones waste away...
> But I trust in you, O Lord;
> I say: "You are my God"; my times are in your
> hand...
> Let your face shine upon your servant;
> save me in your steadfast love.
> Do not let me be put to shame, O Lord,
> for I call on you.
>
> —Psalm 31:1-2, 9-10, 14-17

Again, all of us can identify with the Psalmist here. At times we have felt that life is demanding more than we can possibly give. Whether it be chronic physical pain, the burdens of sorrow, the loss of loved ones, the shame of failure—we feel depleted, our strength ebbing away. Yet we do not lose hope. We turn to the God who has sustained us through so many trials before: "I trust in you, O Lord. Save me in your steadfast love."

## A Psalm of Complaint

The Jewish people have always believed that God wants us to bring ourselves to prayer exactly as we are—no phoniness, no

**25**

cover-ups, no need to launder our words. We can even bring our angry complaints to God. Following is a psalm wherein the believer is struggling with the problem, "Why do the good guys seem to finish last?"

> My steps had nearly slipped.
> For I was envious of the arrogant;
> I saw the prosperity of the wicked.
> For they have no pain; their bodies are sound and
>     sleek.
> They are not in trouble as others are;
> they are not plagued like other people...
> Such are the wicked; always at ease, they increase
>     in riches.
> All in vain I have kept my heart clean,
>     and washed my hands in innocence.
> For all day long I have been plagued,
>     and am punished every morning.
>                                     —Psalm 73:2-5, 12-14

Doesn't that sound like us when we feel we've been cheated by life? We wonder why God allows some people to get away with all kinds of wrongdoing, while so many good people seem to suffer more than their share of life's hardships. Like the Psalmist, we wonder if it "pays" to be virtuous and centered in God. Now is not the time or place to go into a theology of suffering. My only point here is that believers have always felt free to question God, to give voice to their feelings of weariness and even rebellion—precisely because they believed that God was a friend with whom they could be honest. As we saw in the first chapter, prayer is founded on the truth that we are in relationship with God. And prayer is a primary way of growing in that relationship, even when prayer takes the form of lament or complaint.

If we keep reading to the end of Psalm 73, however, we find that the psalmist did not stay stuck in resentment. He or she moved on beautifully to surrender and trust:

Whom have I in heaven but you?
And there is nothing on earth that I desire
more than you.
My flesh and my heart may fail,
but God is the strength of my heart and my
portion forever.

—Psalm 73:25-26

I suspect it took the psalmist some time and some perseverance in prayer to move from the negative state to the positive. That is an important clue for us. Sometimes we have to give vent to our feelings or remain in trustful silence until we can finally come to peace. But in any case, we do not need to put up a front for God. If we are heavy with discouragement, if we're smoldering with resentment, if we're feeling lustful or lonely, if we want revenge—whatever our emotional state—we can bring it all to God in prayer. God sees it all anyway, but that divine knowledge is healing, not intimidating. As the author of the letter to the Hebrews urged: "Let us therefore approach the throne of grace with boldness, so that we may receive mercy and find grace in time of need" (Hebrews 4:16).

### A "Last Resort"
Traditional and formula prayers are gifts to us on our spiritual journey. When we don't know how or what to say to God—when "words fail us"—we Catholics draw upon simple, familiar forms of prayer that we learned at our mother's knee, or during our religious education, or from the ancient words of the biblical Psalms.

We possess a rich treasury indeed.

## Questions for Reflection or Discussion

1. What is your favorite traditional or formula prayer? Why?

2. What do you do when a prayer becomes too familiar or predictable? How do you make it fresh and meaningful again?

3. Have you ever prayed the rosary? If so, what did you like/dislike about it?

4. How familiar are you with the Psalms? Open your Bible to the Psalms and find one that speaks to you.

5. Name some of the other prayers that are in your personal treasury of traditional or formula prayers.

---

### Prayer Activity

Do your own meditation on the Lord's Prayer. Take each phrase and write a few sentences about what it means to you right now. (Do not worry about scriptural or theological accuracy. Write from your heart.)

---

*Chapter Three*

# Conversational Prayer

We often hear of a distinction spiritual writers make between "vocal" prayer and "mental" prayer. In the former we make use of words to address God. In the latter we connect with God through our mind rather than with words. "Formula prayer," as we described in the previous chapter, is an example of vocal prayer.

But another form of vocal prayer familiar to most Catholics is "conversational prayer." Here we talk to God mostly in our own words, without using memorized prayers or prayers composed by others. If prayer is simply a form of communication with God, then surely just talking with God in our own words is an excellent way of praying. Speaking from the heart is one of the most powerful ways to create and sustain intimacy, as any happily married couple or member of a religious community can testify. So, when we pray to God in a conversational style, we are building our relationship with God.

Joyce Rupp, in *Praying Our Goodbyes,* reminds us that our conversation with God can happen anywhere, anytime. Sometimes we speak, sometimes we listen, and sometimes much is communicated without many words being exchanged. No matter how or where we talk with God, Rupp says, "The truth is that God is deeply involved in our lives, touching us with love."

Many of us are already engaging in conversational prayer every day: the parent rocking a baby and thanking God for this precious little gift, the businessperson who asks God in the midst of a tense meeting for the strength to stand firm on ethical practices, commuters who offer spontaneous prayers for their loved ones on the way to or from work, a young person praying fervently for help in a test or athletic event.

Let us reflect a little more at length on two kinds of conversational prayer: petition and thanksgiving.

## Prayers of Petition

Also known as "intercessory prayer," this is probably one of the first forms of prayer we learned as children. "Let's ask God to give us a safe trip," our parents told us as we all bowed our heads in prayer. Or, "Grandpa is going to the hospital for an operation—let's pray for him," they would say. Sometimes they would lead us in an Our Father or a Hail Mary. Other times they might offer a spontaneous prayer.

Most of us caught on quickly and formed the habit of praying for various blessings: to recover from an illness, to get into college, to find a job, to meet someone who could share our life with us. Sometimes our prayers were granted, other times not. Perhaps, if we were disappointed too often, we quit praying.

Sometimes, too, honest doubts may have crossed our minds. We heard people disparaging "gimme" prayers as somehow unworthy of us (or of God): Why not just accept whatever God sends us? Besides, doesn't God already know what we need before we ask? Or we wondered if prayers of petition were merely superstitious ways of trying to manipulate God.

I wrestled with some of these doubts myself. What finally helped me to understand the validity of prayers of petition was the teaching of Jesus. Several times in the gospels he makes it clear that God wants us to pray for what we need. He doesn't give any profound rationale. He just says, "Ask, and it will be given you; search, and you will find; knock, and the door will be opened for you.... Is there anyone among you who, if your child asks for a fish, will give a snake instead of a fish? Or if the child asks for an egg, will give a scorpion? If you then, who are evil, know how to give good gifts to your children, how much more will the heavenly Father give the Holy Spirit to those who ask him!" (Luke 11:9-13).

Underlying this teaching of Jesus, it seems to me, is a profound truth. For even though God obviously knows our needs, we may not always acknowledge them and our dependence on God for their fulfillment. So, in our prayers of petition, we are engaging in two important tasks: one, we are getting in touch with our needs and giving verbal expression to them; and two, we are affirming our belief that "every perfect gift, is from above, coming down from the Father of lights" (James 1:17).

Something else you will notice in Jesus' teaching: He never says that we will receive exactly what we pray for. What he does promise is that we will receive the Holy Spirit. The promise is that "your Father in heaven (will) give good things to those who ask him" (Matthew 7:11). Years ago I heard Jesuit Father David Stanley make a statement I have never forgotten. He said there is an "infallible promise" Jesus gives us here: *that every sincere prayer of ours will be heard and granted by God.* Again, this is not a guarantee that we will receive exactly what we asked for. The experience of most of us has proved otherwise. But, as the text from Matthew says, we will always receive "good things." That is, God will give us what we truly need, though it may not be what we wanted or asked for.

For we Christians believe that God is only capable of giving good gifts. Perhaps the lesson is even clearer in the same passage from Luke: "How much more will the heavenly Father give *the Holy Spirit* to those who ask" (Luke 11:13). Thus, when we make any sincere prayer of petition—even if the particular request is not granted—we will always receive the Spirit of love, the Spirit of union with God. The bond of relationship between ourselves and God will thus always be strengthened, and that is the primary purpose of any and all prayer. How good it is to know that our prayers of petition, even when we aren't sure how or what to pray for, will have an unfailing spiritual effect in our lives.

### What Can We Pray For?

Note that I used the modifier *sincere* when speaking of intercessory prayer. What do I mean by that? It has to do with the question: What should we pray for? My answer is that we should pray for anything that is worthy of a child of God. That would exclude things that are not worthy of us at our best. For instance, I should not pray that some misfortune happen to someone I don't like, or that my conscience won't bother me when I sin, or that all terrorists will go to hell. But should I pray to do well in school, or regain my health, or find a good marriage partner? Of course. These are all things "worthy of a child

**31**

of God." Likewise, we can pray for all sorts of "good things" for other people: healing for illness, peace in the family, a good future for our children, finding a job, an end to war and violence, improved life for those who are impoverished. This is what we do at the Prayer of the Faithful at every Mass, and we are encouraged to do so in our private prayers as well.

I keep remembering other instances in the gospels where Jesus instructs us about intercessory prayer. Once, when Jesus was absent, a man brought his son to the disciples and asked them to expel the evil spirit from him. But they were unable to do so. When Jesus arrived on the scene, he promptly cured the boy of his affliction. When the disciples asked, "Why couldn't we cast it out?" Jesus answered, "This kind can come out only through prayer" (see Mark 9:14-29). The disciples, apparently, had neglected to take that first step: earnestly and persistently asking God to do what they were incapable of accomplishing through their own limited powers.

Speaking of persistence, Jesus also gave his disciples a parable "about their need to pray always and not to lose heart" (Luke 18:1). He told the delightful story of a poor widow who kept pestering an uncaring judge to hear her case against an unjust opponent. Finally, the judge says in exasperation: "Though I have no fear of God and no respect for anyone, yet because this widow keeps bothering me, I will grant her justice, so that she may not wear me out" (Luke 18:4-5). How much more, Jesus says, will God hear the prayers of his beloved ones "who cry to him day and night?" (Luke 18:1-8).

In this connection I am always reminded of the *Peanuts* cartoon where Linus finds his sister Lucy on her knees in prayer. "What were you praying for?" he asks. Lucy says, "I was praying for patience—but I quit!" Not quite the right attitude, Jesus would say.

We need to be persistent and persevering in our prayer—not so much for God's sake but for our own. If something is really important to us, we will not quit praying for it just because we don't get a quick answer. Sometimes I have had to pray for years before my prayer was granted. Was it worth it? Absolutely. I have no doubt that many of you have had the same experience.

## Prayers of Thanksgiving

The other common form of conversational prayer is the prayer of gratitude. One of our earliest lessons in social graces is to say "Thank you" when someone gives us a gift. Even more so, we were taught, when it comes to the gifts of God: We can't keep begging for things without ever saying thanks for what we have already received.

There seems to be some kind of warped tendency in human nature to take things for granted. Or maybe this is true only in a society of abundance like our own—what someone once called the "utter availability of everything." As a result of our blessings we may drift into an attitude of entitlement, like the nine-year-old boy Ann Landers once quoted. One night at the family meal he announced, "I'm running away from home tomorrow. Who's going to drive me?" So, too, we may come to expect that nearly everything in life, rather than being a precious gift, is somehow owed to us.

That was not the mind-set of our ancestors in the faith. In the Old Testament it is clear that devout Jews lived in an atmosphere of gratitude. They were in awe at the wonders of God's power in creation and at the goodness and mercy that God constantly extended toward human creatures. The only appropriate response was prayer—the prayer of praise and thanksgiving. Here is a beautiful example of this:

> Bless the Lord, O my soul,
> and all that is within me, bless his holy name.
> Bless the Lord, O my soul,
> and do not forget all his benefits—
> who forgives all your iniquity,
> who heals all your diseases,
> who redeems your life from the Pit,
> who crowns you with steadfast love and mercy,
> who satisfies you with good as long as you live,
> so that your youth is renewed like the eagle's.
> —Psalm 103:1-5

I often say, only half-jokingly: "Children and adolescents are constitutionally incapable of gratitude!" Indeed, I have a hunch that growth in gratitude is a normal developmental process that is aided by a big helping of divine grace. As we mature, most of us are less likely to take things for granted, more likely to both feel and express gratitude. We come to recognize that much of life is terribly fragile. This is why the date of September 11, 2001, has been burned into our collective memory forever. We now realize (if we didn't before) that we never know when we or our loved ones may die, when the economy is going to slump, when downsizing and job cuts will hit us. So we have come to treasure the gift of life, to appreciate good health, to be grateful for family, for friends, for all that makes life beautiful. And we bring all that to our prayer. Our prayers of thanks become as frequent and heartfelt as our prayers of petition.

One of the truly heroic figures in my life has been Father Solanus Casey, a fellow Capuchin from my province. For years he exercised a wonderful healing ministry in New York and Detroit, and his cause for canonization is now pending in Rome. He was a man who lived in a constant spirit of gratitude. His favorite expression was "Thanks be to God!" Another was "Blessed be God in all his designs." One of the most frequent words found in his speech and his letters was "appreciate." For Father Solanus, absolutely everything was a gift from God. In fact, he would urge people coming to him for help to "thank God ahead of time" for what God was *going* to do for them. For even if they did not receive what they asked for, Solanus believed, "the good God" (another of his favorite expressions) would surely give them some gift or grace in answer to their prayers.

Prayers of gratitude sometimes take the form of praise. Indeed, praise and thanks are practically interchangeable in the vocabulary of prayer. In praise, we honor God for all the attributes that are proper to the divine: creative power, profound wisdom, unconditional love, inexhaustible mercy, compassion for the poor and afflicted. And in our prayer, we often join the two together: "Our God, we praise and thank you for...."

## Praying Our Daily Experiences

We have been talking about various forms of conversational prayer, wherein we simply talk to God in our own words. I would like to conclude this chapter by describing a method of conversational prayer that unites both thanksgiving and petition.

I discovered this way of praying some years ago in an article by Jesuit Father George Maloney, and I adapted it for my own use in prayer. It closely resembles a prayer form developed by another Jesuit, Father George Aschenbrenner, that he calls "Consciousness Examen." It is the format I use most frequently myself.

I begin the prayer by briefly asking God to walk with me through the previous day and to help me view it with the eyes of faith. Then I review in my mind the events of the previous day. First I give thanks for whatever was positive, uplifting, inspiring: "Lord God, thank you so much for the good phone conversation I had with my sister yesterday. She's starting to feel better again, she had a nice Thanksgiving with her daughters and their families, and we had some good laughs. And thank you for the liturgies I celebrated at the parish I visited this weekend. I had never been there before, and the people were warm and friendly to me. The music was wonderful; the people sang, even at the early Mass. I felt good about my preaching, and I sensed people were being touched. I thoroughly enjoyed Saturday night dinner with the pastor. Thank you for good priests like him." I continue to reflect on the day and to give thanks for other ways the Lord gifted me—including the fact that I got home safely despite the rotten weather.

Then I will recall those moments or events where I was negligent or irresponsible or self-centered or just plain sinful. I ask for forgiveness and the grace to correct those kinds of failures. Sometimes, of course, it has been a particularly difficult day. Some people I dealt with may have been uncooperative or even nasty. A couple of things (some days, practically everything!) might have gone wrong: I couldn't find something; my phone call wasn't returned; my brilliant advice was dismissed; I felt hurt by some criticism that got back to me third- or fourth-

**35**

hand.

Next I spend some time talking to God about this stuff. If I was at fault, I try to admit it and pray for the grace of conversion. If other people were at fault, I ask for the grace to forgive them. If it was just bad luck or circumstance, I ask God to somehow redeem the situation and bring some good out of it. I pray for God to teach me what I'm supposed to learn from the day. (That way, I believe, even a perfectly bad day doesn't get wasted!)

And finally, I look ahead to the coming day. I ask God to help me with the tasks on my agenda and with my ministry to people. If I am worried about something coming up that day, I ask for guidance and strength to deal with it: "Lord, I've got to start planning that retreat day for the parish. I've been procrastinating too long already. I'm just not sure what direction to go with it. Please help me to get a focus and to inspire the people with the message that *you* want them to receive."

I won't pretend that my conversational prayer is always fervent and soul-satisfying. But the method is not difficult, and most of the time I find nourishment in this kind of prayer. But there are other ways to pray, and we will continue to explore these in the coming chapters.

## Questions for Reflection or Discussion

1. What are the positives of conversational prayer for you? What are the negatives, if any?

2. Have you ever had a prayer of petition answered? Were your prayers ever answered in a way that you did not expect? Describe what happened.

3. What do you feel you should pray for? Are there any things that you feel you should not pray for? Why?

4. Recall the last prayer of thanksgiving you made. What were the circumstances? How did you feel afterwards?

5. Describe what a conversation with God is like for you. Who speaks first? What do you talk about? How long does it last? What, if anything, gets "accomplished"?

---

### Prayer Activity

Make your own "Consciousness Examen." Ask God to walk with you through the previous day and help you view it with the eyes of faith. Give thanks for what was positive, uplifting, inspiring. Then recall those moments or events where you were negligent or irresponsible or self-centered or sinful. Ask for forgiveness and the grace to correct your failures. Next, talk to God about everything. Ask God to teach you what you are supposed to learn from the day. Finally, look ahead to the coming day and ask God to help you.

---

*Chapter Four*

# Praying with the Bible

It is no secret that we Catholics generally do not know the Bible as well as our Protestant brothers and sisters, but that has been changing since the Second Vatican Council. The Council urged us to draw upon the treasures of scripture to nourish our life of faith and of prayer. This is why the celebration of the Mass and all the sacraments have been revised to emphasize reading and reflection on scripture. Moreover, contemporary spiritual writers keep providing us with abundant ways to use the Bible for our personal prayer.

For centuries monastic communities and other groups have made use of a prayer form called *lectio divina* (holy reading). It consists of reading (or listening to) a passage from scripture, usually repeated several times. Then the participants reflect silently upon the word of God, turning it over in their minds, connecting it with their own lives, and offering conversational prayers in silence. The idea is that the word of God entering our hearts is like the seed that "fell into good soil and brought forth grain" (Mark 4:8). It begins to take root in us, offer us instruction, give us God's perspective on ourselves and the events of our lives. It inspires us with courage and with trust in the power and goodness of God. It challenges our sinful ways and invites us to conversion. It reveals the blessings God has already poured out upon us and calls us to be thankful.

We need to be clear that the Bible is not just about the past. It would be easy to dismiss scripture by saying, "That stuff all happened a long time ago. It has nothing to do with my life now." If that were true, the Bible would have stopped selling a long time ago. Why does it continue to outrank all other books in total sales? The answer is that its stories and truths are timeless. I have been conducting a series of evenings for men entitled "Men of the Bible." I simply tell the stories of great male biblical figures—Abraham, Jacob, Joseph, David, Jeremiah, Peter and Paul—and try to show how they were a blend of strength and weakness, nobility and nastiness, greatness of soul and pettiness. I am touched at how the men make the connections, see themselves in the stories, and draw spiritual inspiration from them. Many writers and speakers are doing the same with the Bible's female characters.

When we start to dig into the Bible we find that it addresses the deepest questions of the human heart: Who am I? What is the purpose of my life? Where is my center—the base from which my decisions flow? What is God's plan for human happiness? Our minds are hungry for the truth. The Bible teaches us the truth about ourselves and about the world we live in. It teaches us how to become "the best we can be."

The other conviction we need to have is that the Bible is not just a human word but the word of God. As we saw in the first chapter, God takes the initiative in communicating with us. One of the ways is through the great themes of scripture. We also saw that God's initiative calls for response on our part. In this case, our response is to listen to God's word in order to acquire the divine vision of reality.

### A Method of Praying with Scripture

Because praying with scripture has such a long tradition in the church, I want to explore it with a little more depth. In the first place, this kind of prayer is not something we rush into. What we do immediately before we pray in this manner is important. We must spend a few minutes quieting ourselves down, relaxing and letting go of our preoccupations. We need to recall that God is present to us in a personal way at this very moment and ask to be open to receive whatever gift the Lord wants to give us during this prayer time.

Next we select a scripture passage for reading and reflection. There are different ways of doing this. If we have a daily missal or our parish bulletin lists the daily readings, we can use the scripture passages for the Mass of that day. Or we can take one of the gospels, or any other book of the Bible, and read a few verses. Usually five to ten verses are enough, but we should not break up a complete story or unit.

Then we read the passage through once, just to get a feel for it as a whole. We note the words or phrases that strike us, or the general theme or point of the passage. Then we go over it slowly and reflectively, trying to see the connections between these words of scripture and the concerns we have about ourselves, our loved ones, our world. The questions I always have in the back of my mind are: What truth is God (Jesus) trying to teach me here? How does that truth connect with my life? What response am I being called to make? And I listen carefully for "answers" to those questions. Not that I actually hear the voice of God speaking, but I pay close attention to the thoughts, feelings and intuitions that come to me in the silence.

Sometimes there may be no direct connection with the "stuff" of our life, but we just get a different or deeper insight into the ways of God or into life's larger questions. Often we will be moved to praise God, to offer thanks for blessings ("I had a terrible dream last night and I want to thank you that it was only a dream!"), to ask God for what we or others may need. Sometimes we may want to question God: What does this phrase in scripture mean? How do you want me to deal with so-and-so? Why isn't that project of mine going anywhere? Sometimes we receive an answer; sometimes we don't. (When the latter happens, I always figure God needs some more time to think about it.) We may want to conclude by making some specific requests for ourselves or others and end with the Our Father or some other formula prayer.

Again, the assumption here is that prayer is an act of communication between friends. Here we begin by listening rather than talking. We listen to God addressing us in the words of scripture, and we let that word touch our minds and hearts. Usually we respond by speaking to God in our own words. I want to emphasize again that we can be as free and open with God in prayer as we are with any other friend. If we want to strengthen a relationship with someone, the best and most direct way is to spend time with that person in honest communication.

### An Example of Praying with Scripture

I would like to share with you an example of praying with scripture from my own experience. Some years ago I made a directed retreat at a time when I was coming off of some painful experiences. The first day I met with my director, he asked me to pray over a passage from Isaiah. As I did so, I made notes of my reflections. I share them with you as an example of how we might pray with scripture.

First, here is the scripture passage in its entirety:

Ho, everyone who thirsts,
    come to the waters;
and you that have no money,
    come, buy and eat!
Come, buy wine and milk
    without money and without price.
Why do you spend your money for that which is
        not bread,
    and your labor for that which does not satisfy?
Listen carefully to me, and eat what is good,
    and delight yourselves in rich food.
Incline your ear, and come to me;
    listen, so that you may live.
I will make with you an everlasting covenant,
    my steadfast, sure love for David.
See, I made him a witness to the peoples,
    a leader and commander for the peoples.
See, you shall call nations that you do not know,
    and nations that do not know you shall run to
        you,
because of the LORD your God, the Holy One of
        Israel,
    for he has glorified you.

Seek the LORD while he may be found,
    call upon him while he is near;
let the wicked forsake their way,
    and the unrighteous their thoughts;

let them return to the LORD, that he may have
    mercy on them,
and to our God, for he will abundantly pardon.
For my thoughts are not your thoughts,
    nor are your ways my ways, says the LORD.
For as the heavens are higher than the earth,
    so are my ways higher than your ways
and my thoughts than your thoughts.

For as the rain and the snow come down from
    heaven,
and do not return there until they have watered
    the earth,
making it bring forth and sprout,
    giving seed to the sower and bread to the eater,
so shall my word be that goes out from my mouth;
    it shall not return to me empty,
but it shall accomplish that which I purpose,
    and succeed in the thing for which I sent it.
                                    —Isaiah 55:1-11

The first thing I notice in this passage is how often God
says "come" and "listen." How passionately God pursues us—
not out of need for us but simply because God desires our happiness so strongly and knows how easily we tend to look for it
somewhere else.

Everyone who thirsts, come to the waters;
    and you that have no money, come, buy and eat!
Come, buy wine and milk
    without money and without price.

I've certainly come to this retreat "thirsty." I was not
enthused about coming. It seemed like one more "should" in
my life. But now that I'm here, I realize how hungry and thirsty
I am. I can hardly get enough of scripture—and of solitude.
"Come, without paying and without cost." It struck me what a
luxury this retreat is. How many people can take six days out of

their schedule to do nothing but take stock of their life in the light of God's word? Again I feel gratitude.

> Why do you spend your money for that which is
> not bread,
> and your labor for that which does not satisfy?

How true these lines are. Sunday I spent a lot of money to play golf, and all it did was depress me. That's only a symbol of what I keep doing to myself over and over. It's not so much the money as the squandered time and the false expectations. I constantly think this or that will satisfy me, but it never does. The next verse tells me what will:

> Listen carefully to me, and eat what is good...
> Incline your ear and come to me;
> Listen, so you may live.

This leads me to my prayer practices. Lord, you know I've been quite faithful in devoting time to prayer, but I fear it's become another "should." I don't come to you "carefully," really expecting to be filled. I need to reflect more on this: How can I come to prayer with a more receptive, positive attitude?

> Seek the Lord while he may be found,
> call upon him while he is near.

These lines strike me as odd, Lord. Can't you always be "found"? Aren't you always "near"? What's the urgency? Maybe it has something to do with passion. If you are passionate in seeking me, shouldn't my response be similar? If I don't seek you while you are near, if I seek you only half-heartedly or as an "also-ran," am I not in danger of losing you (or at least rendering you remote and harmless)? In any case, I know how laid-back I can become about seeking you and how I spend passion on "what fails to satisfy."

For my thoughts are not your thoughts,
    nor are your ways my ways, says the Lord.
For as the heavens are higher than the earth,
    so are my ways higher than your ways,
    and my thoughts than your thoughts.

This says that the wicked must forsake their ways and the unrighteous their thoughts. But the text also implies that all of us need to submit our thoughts and ways to God's. It's strange, but I find more comfort than challenge in that. Lord, I'm glad that my thoughts and ways are not the last word, the final measure of reality. The challenge is to keep measuring them against yours. But the comfort is that even when my perception of something is skewed or I meet with apparent failure, it may not be so in your eyes. Your ways are above mine. You can see farther and clearer. Once again, I am called to do what I honestly think best and then leave the outcome to you.

For as the rain and the snow
    come down from heaven and do not return there
until they have watered the earth,
    making it bring forth and sprout,
giving seed to the sower and bread to the eater,
    so shall my word be that goes out from my
        mouth;
it shall not return to me empty,
    but it shall accomplish that which I purpose,
and succeed in the thing for which I sent it.

I recall how the ancients thought of time as a repetitive cycle that goes nowhere. This passage gives a totally different vision: God's word breaks in and has an impact—on history and in our daily lives. I need to hold on to this truth, Lord. I can get pessimistic and cynical about the state of the world and the church. Sometimes it seems like the gospel of Jesus doesn't have a chance. I want to believe that your word "shall not return to you empty" but shall accomplish your purpose. I never know when and how this is going to happen. So often I've been amazed that people were touched by what I thought was a trite, obvious statement I had made—or by something I didn't even remember saying. Your word, Lord, is both weak and powerful at the same time. My job is to give it every chance to be heard. Again I'm reminded of Cardinal Newman's prayer: "God does nothing in vain. He knows what he is about.... Therefore I will trust him."

Please don't get the idea that things flow as neatly as the above every time I sit down to pray. Far from it. Most of the time my thoughts and prayers are a jumbled mess. But that need not discourage us. God really does accept us wherever we are at the time we pray. We certainly will not come to new truths or insights each time. Sometimes we will just receive a deeper understanding or appreciation of what we already believe. But that, too, is a valuable gift. And sometimes the only response God wants of us is adoration, gratitude or a deeper desire to know the divine will. That is enough.

### *Fruits of Scriptural Prayer*
What are the benefits of praying with scripture? The most obvious, perhaps, is a greater familiarity with the Bible. As we said before, many Catholics do not know the Bible very well, largely because they were not encouraged or instructed on how to read it. But when we start using the Bible for personal prayer, we begin to feel at home with it. For one thing, we are surprised to discover how many popular sayings have their origins in the Bible: "like a lost sheep," "O ye of little faith," "a thief in the night," "my brother's keeper," "the handwriting on the wall."

But more importantly, if we pray with scripture, the readings at Mass will begin to speak to us more clearly, because our prayer has been tuned in to biblical themes and images. We will find ourselves listening more attentively to the readings and to the homily. We will have acquired a hunger and thirst—an appetite—for the word of God. We may even develop a desire to share our reflections on the word with family members or with other people. We may search for commentaries and other books to help us understand scripture better. All of this contributes to our spiritual growth.

Perhaps most significant of all, praying with scripture can give us a deeper understanding of the purpose of life. Prayer calls us to examine our ways: Who shapes my vision? Whose values have I chosen to embody? Who has authority over my mind and my choices—my peers or coworkers, talk show hosts and their guests, current celebrities, the majority in the opinion polls, the hottest authors of the moment?

Christians have always claimed to have a different vision of life than the one propounded by the society around them. In his book *Call to Conversion,* Jim Wallis notes that the First Letter of Peter took it for granted that unbelievers would notice something different about Christians and would ask them why they live the way they do: "Always be ready to make your defense to anyone who demands from you an accounting for the hope that is in you; yet do it with gentleness and reverence" (1 Peter 3:15). How come, Wallis wonders, nobody asks us questions about our faith anymore? Most likely it is because we modern Christians live pretty much the same as everyone else. There's nothing different about our lifestyle, so presumably there's nothing different about our vision or belief system.

In other words, perhaps without realizing it we have allowed our vision and our values to be shaped by something other than the biblical vision. The gospel of Jesus Christ is in fierce competition with the "gospel" of the prevailing culture: the gospel of upward mobility, of acquisition and consumption, of self-gratification, of wielding power and influence, of blindness to the needs of the poor and disadvantaged. I don't think we realize deeply enough how much our culture affects us. It is in the very air we breathe. It finds expression in so many places: in advertising, in movies and television shows, in self-help books, in public policies.

So here we have another important reason for praying with the Bible. We need an alternative to the prevailing values of our culture. We want to know God's vision for the good life, and that vision is revealed first of all in the Bible, especially in the life and teachings of Jesus Christ. The Bible is the privileged instrument for the revelation of God's design for our temporal and eternal happiness.

Finally, let me finish with a word of caution. Praying with scripture can become an intellectual exercise or head trip rather than prayer. Because the meaning of biblical texts is not always self-evident, we may find ourselves puzzling over a word or passage rather than praying. Some Bibles have excellent footnotes that can clarify the text, or we may invest in a biblical commentary to help us. But the bottom line is that praying with scripture is about attending to the presence of God, not studying some ancient texts. I wish to stress again that the purpose of prayer is to grow in our relationship with God. If praying with scripture does not do that for us, we should feel free to drop it. Let us not mistake the means for the end. As we will see, there are still plenty of other forms of prayer that have nourished Catholics over the centuries.

### Questions for Reflection or Discussion

1. Have you ever prayed with scripture? What was the result? Did you enjoy it? Why or why not?

2. If you have prayed with scripture (or even if you have never tried it), what do you think would be your favorite book of the Bible to use? Why?

3. Take the Bible and flip it open at random. Now read until you find a passage that speaks to you. Read it aloud.

4. Do you agree that the Bible presents a very different set of values than are currently popular in our culture? Give some examples.

5. Try to recall a scripture reading that was read at a Mass or other liturgical celebration you attended. What struck you about the reading? Why did it stick in your mind?

## Prayer Activity

Pick a passage from the Bible, either a random one or one of your favorites. Following the example in this chapter, break the passage down into segments and speak with God about how each segment might apply to your daily life.

*Chapter Five*

# Meditation and Contemplation

So far we have been talking about "vocal" prayer, wherein we communicate with God verbally, using the words of others or those of our own. In this chapter we will consider two forms of what is often called "mental" prayer for the simple reason that it is prayed most often (though not exclusively) with our mind and heart, without the use of spoken words. The first of these prayer methods is usually termed *meditation*, while the second is called *contemplation*.

Meditation has moved from the monasteries into popular culture. Courses in yoga and meditation have sprung up everywhere. Corporations pay big money for workshops on meditation for their executives and many have added "meditation rooms" to their office suites and complexes.

What's going on? Quite simply, physiologists and psychologists have discovered that meditation, as practiced by monks and spiritual masters for centuries, has beneficial effects on the human mind and body. It reduces stress by lowering heart rate and blood pressure, inducing muscular relaxation, reducing stress and gently toning the entire nervous system.

Catholics are not surprised at this. We know that our mind, body and spirit form a wondrous unit. We value wholistic health as much as anyone. But we insist that meditation is not just a way to reduce stress or to increase productivity. It is, first of all, prayer. Its proper object is God. Its goal is deepening our relationship with the divine. So we need to look at meditation as a spiritual discipline, a form of prayer.

### What Is Meditation?

I will not give a strict definition of meditation but rather a description. Meditation is a way of prayer in which we focus on some divine truth or mystery. We employ our imagination and our reason to reflect on a scene from the Bible, or on one of the church's teachings, or on some truth of our faith. But meditation, to be true prayer, does not remain in the head. It includes our feelings and our will. We allow ourselves to be emotionally moved by our meditation, and we give expression to our affections by nonverbal expressions of praise, gratitude, wonder, repentance and perhaps even by making a decision or choice of action. Sometimes we will use words to express these sentiments, and in that sense meditation includes some elements of vocal prayer. Still, most of our prayer happens in our minds and without words.

Let us consider an example. Say it's the Christmas season, and you heard a homily on the text "The Word became flesh and lived among us" (John 1:14). Later that day, you take some time to meditate on that text. You begin with a short prayer for God's help and guidance. You quiet yourself and place yourself consciously in God's presence. Then you begin to reflect. You recall what the preacher said. The words *lived among us* literally mean (in the original Greek) "pitched his tent among us." This recalls the Exodus through the desert, where God "dwelt" with the Israelites through the symbol of the Ark of the Covenant, which was housed in a tent in the midst of the people's tents.

"Wow!" you say to yourself. "God was trying to tell the Israelites how close the divine presence was to them, how intimately God wanted to share their lives and their hardships. And now God has come into the world in the humble form of a small child."

You think of the child in the manger, stretching out his arms to us as if to say, "I want to be here with you, to dwell with you, to share your life and everything it involves."

You answer: "Lord Jesus, I'm seeing now that the message is not just generic. You mean it for me personally. You want to be part of *my* life, *my* family, *my* work, *my* friendships. I want to welcome you, not shut you out. But what would that really mean?"

At this point you might spend some more time reflecting on that question. You would think, for example, of how you sometimes fail to see Christ in your family or coworkers, or how you do not always reveal the love of Christ to them, or how you rely entirely too much on your own resources and do not ask Christ to help you deal with situations in a truly spiritual way. And then you might ask forgiveness and pray for the grace to be more mindful of that wonderful "Word-made-flesh" dwelling within you and around you. Finally, you may end by making some decision: "I've been neglecting one of my sons lately because he seems so sullen. I'm going to invite him to join me for pizza and try to engage him in conversation. Lord, please help me to find the right words—and above all, the right attitude."

Here, by the way, is an example of what I said in the first chapter: Prayer can be "dangerous." It can lead us into actions or places that we would just as soon avoid. So the above meditation starts out with a nice warm Christmas image and ends with a decision that involves risk—and possibly rejection or failure. But how else can we grow spiritually, except by stretching ourselves—or letting ourselves be stretched by God?

### Guided Meditation

It may have struck you that the above example of meditation looks a lot like "Praying with scripture" as described in the previous chapter. There certainly are similarities. The difference is that meditation can take a wider variety of forms. It need not be scripture-based. For instance, we might choose to meditate on the brilliant colors of autumn, or a falling leaf, or a statement or question we heard from a child that really made us think, or the beautiful philosophy of life we heard from a person we visited in a nursing home. Somehow these experiences touch us and call us to prayer. So we turn them over in our mind, try to see the connections between them and our faith, and offer spontaneous prayers of adoration, thanksgiving, contrition and intercession.

A number of fine books have been written as aids for meditation. For instance, Isaias Powers has one called *Quiet Places With Jesus: 40 Guided Imagery Meditations for Personal Prayer.* "Guided meditations" or "guided imagery" are ways of helping us meditate. They generally present us with a scene from the Bible and invite us to place ourselves within that scene as if we were a spectator or a participant. Then they suggest possible dialogues between ourselves and one of the biblical figures, usually Jesus. For example, Powers has one called "The Courage of Jesus—Ours for the Asking." He has us picture Jesus as he experienced rejection from the townsfolk of Nazareth where he grew up. As they became more enraged at him and threatened to hurl him over the cliff, Jesus remained steadfast and would not back down on what he had said about their tendency to reject the prophets sent to them. Then he walked through their midst and went on his way (see Luke 4:20-30).

Powers then suggests that we think of people in our own lives who try to intimidate us or turn us away from our intended goals. He recommends we picture ourselves standing at the edge of the cliff and wanting to end it all. "Then notice Jesus," he says, "walking down toward you from a higher hill.... Wait for him—do not look down! Do not think about leaping into despair.... Let Jesus take your hand.... Let his courage be passed on to you; feel the warmth of it coming from his hand; feel the weight on your shoulders lighten; feel the spring in your steps come back." As is evident, meditations like these are largely nonverbal. They draw upon our memory and imagination to evoke strong religious or spiritual feelings in us. There is little need for words, though some people may be moved to pray with words. But essentially, the stirring up of the emotions and the deeper awareness of God's presence are themselves the prayer.

Another form of guided meditation is "going to your favorite place." It is often done in groups during a retreat, but it may also be done individually. In a group setting we are asked to take a comfortable position, place ourselves in an atmosphere of sacred silence, and close our eyes.

A leader then directs our imagination along these lines:

> Picture yourself walking leisurely toward your
> favorite place. It may be a spot in the woods, on a
> beach, on a hill or mountain, in a church or chapel, in

your own backyard. Imagine yourself going to that place by way of a path in the woods. It's a bright, glorious day with blue skies and sunlight forming patterns of light and shadow on the path. Along the path you notice wildflowers, and your heart is full with the beauty of God's creation.

Suddenly the path takes a turn, and you are in your favorite place. You spread a blanket and sit down, just drinking in the goodness of the moment. After being there alone for a while in the quiet, you become aware of another presence. You look up, and find yourself looking into the face of Jesus. You notice his face, and how he is dressed. You don't know what to say, how to act. But he breaks the tension with a gentle smile. And then he looks straight at you and says, "How are you doing?"

The invitation is so genuine, so heartfelt, that you want to tell him. Not in conventional or superficial terms, but with all honesty—your positive feelings as well as your doubts, struggles and burdens. So now, go ahead and talk to him—in the silence of your mind and heart....

Now Jesus looks lovingly at you again and says, "Thank you for entrusting all that to me. But now— what would you like me to do for you? What gift do you think you need at this time?" Take some time to think about that; then tell him. But when you're finished, spend some listening to what Jesus wants to say to you.

As you would imagine, guided meditations can be a powerful form of prayer. People are sometimes crying at the end. For some it may be the first time they have felt free and comfortable enough to talk to Christ person-to-person. Others are surprised to discover long-buried thoughts and feelings that they can finally face and deal with. For others this prayer form is simply another way they can deepen their relationship with the Lord.

## Contemplative Moments

First, don't let the word *contemplative* scare you off. Too often we think that only cloistered monks and nuns and those we call mystics can practice contemplative prayer. The truth is, contemplation is a very ancient form of prayer that many ordinary people have practiced over the centuries.

What can happen is this. We may reach a point in our life where we experience blocking, stagnation or dissatisfaction with our usual ways of praying: formula prayer, praying with scripture, meditation, whatever. We are puzzled and discouraged. We don't know what to do. We may be tempted to give up prayer entirely. If we are fortunate, someone tells us about contemplative prayer and the fact that it is a normal form of Christian prayer. We learn more about it, try it, and discover ourselves able to pray again.

I would describe contemplative prayer as a way of communicating with God in the depths of our being—by a simple gaze of love, with very few words or even thoughts. It is clearly a form of "mental" prayer, but it differs from meditation in that our mind is much less active and our emotions are right at the surface. It is "prayer of the heart." Saint Teresa of Ávila called it "the prayer of quiet." Contemporary writers like Thomas Keating and Basil Pennington call it "centering prayer." Others (and this is my favorite term) describe it as "the prayer of simple union."

I believe all of us have had what I would call contemplative moments. That is, we become aware—suddenly or gradually— that we are in the presence of some Being, some Mystery far greater than ourselves. As my Capuchin brother Daniel Crosby likes to put it, "There is something more here than meets the eye." We recognize the mystery as God, present to us in a very real, immediate way.

For instance, have you ever watched the sun setting over an ocean or lake? Not only is it beautiful beyond words, but sometimes we experience a profound sense of union—somehow we are at one with the sun, with the water, with the brilliant sky, with the person next to us—indeed, with the whole human family. And all of it and all of us are connected with the very essence of God. It is not that we are God or "parts" of God (that would be pantheism), but somehow we are at one with God and with all creation. And that is a profoundly serene and joyful feeling.

Something similar can happen when we hold a newborn baby in our arms. We somehow have the total and unshakable conviction (but without any logical "proof") that only God could form such a perfect little creature and in fact is present in the baby itself.

In her book *A Tree Full of Angels,* Macrina Wiederkehr notes the heightened interest nowadays in extraordinary spiritual phenomena such as visions, weeping statues, and rosaries that turn gold. She invites us to gaze instead with the eyes of faith at the hidden presence of God all around us. "The greatest of all visions," she says, "is to see Christ, indeed to see God, in the frail and glorious family of the world."

I remember very vividly one evening when I was writing Christmas cards. I had Beethoven's Seventh Symphony playing in the background and was suddenly overtaken by the music. It touched something deep inside of me, and I felt the power and presence of God in my very soul. My mind recalled that Beethoven was nearly deaf at the time he wrote that symphony. How, I wondered, could he have created such magnificent music out of such deprivation? "Gift of God" was my instant thought. And from there my mind leaped to Christmas. What was Christmas but the ultimate Gift of God? The Son of God came into our world, to be with us in our blindness and our deafness and our loneliness and all the other limitations of our humanity. And he assured us that we are loved and loveable. I realized in the depth of my soul that we all have a God-given dignity that nothing and nobody can take away, even as Beethoven's deafness and disordered personal life could not rob him of his power to create unforgettable music. That experience was fifteen years ago, and it only lasted a few moments, but it was a contemplative moment I will always remember.

### Contemplation as Prayer
Besides such contemplative moments, we may find ourselves

**57**

drawn to contemplative prayer. This consists basically of directing our attention to the presence of God dwelling in our heart. This kind of prayer is grounded in the mystery of our baptism. We do not have to look "outside" for God. We are already bathed and immersed in the divine presence. Theologians speak of the "divine indwelling" that occurs from the moment of our baptism: the three Persons of the Trinity "taking up residence" in the depths of our being. This is not a mere image or figure of speech. It is based on the words of Jesus to the disciples at the Last Supper: "Those who love me will keep my word, and my Father will love them, and we will come to them and make our home with them" (John 14:23). "Make our home"— what warmth and intimacy those words convey!

So if prayer is any act whereby we pay attention to the presence of God within us or around us, then contemplation is a way of paying attention to God dwelling in our soul. It is a remarkably simple process. First, as usual, we take some moments to quiet ourselves, relax our muscles, and breathe deeply. Then we move to the center of our being where God dwells in abiding love. We spend some time just resting in that love.

Next we choose a single word or a phrase that links us to God such as *Father, Mother, Parent, Jesus, Savior, Spirit, Holy One.* It may also be a phrase. It is said that Saint Francis of Assisi would spend the whole night repeating the words, "My God and my All!" From early centuries, Christians of the East have used the Jesus Prayer: "Lord Jesus Christ, Son of the living God, be merciful to me a sinner." They have repeated the prayer over and over, while walking or working in the fields. Other phrases can be drawn from scripture: "I come to you, Lord, for I am weary and burdened" or "Do not be afraid" or "Know that I am with you always" or "Lord, be my strength today." We will find ourselves changing the word or phrase from time to time to revitalize our contemplation.

It is not necessary to keep repeating the word or phrase constantly. The important thing in contemplative prayer is to stay focused on God. Whenever we are distracted or our attention wanders, however, we need but gently return to the sacred word without a lot of anxiety or forcefulness.

This method of contemplation is usually called centering prayer, because its purpose is to help us remain centered in God. As you can see, it is remarkably simple, but it is not easy! I myself do not pray well this way. My mind is too active, so I need something like praying with scripture or praying my daily experiences. Each of us must find the form or forms of prayer that best fits our personality or our mental state at the time. And we should not hesitate to switch methods when one is no longer working for us.

I might add that some people can pray contemplatively without using any words at all. Remember that the essence of this prayer is to attend to the presence of God. There is an old story about the farmer who would stop in the country church every evening after his work in the fields and remain there a long time in prayer. The pastor had noticed that the man never used a book or a rosary and never seemed to move his lips. So one day he asked the peasant, "My son, I am edified by your devotion to prayer. But I wonder what you say to the Lord while you are here praying?" The man replied, "Well, I don't really say anything. I just look at God, and God looks at me." Contemplative prayer is simply a way of seeing, of beholding and delighting in the wonderful mystery of God within us and all around us.

### Praying with the Body

Perhaps this is a good place to mention another aspect of contemplative prayer, that is, praying with our body or "body prayer." Some people have found that they cannot always express their interior faith and relationship with God in words or even thoughts. So they simply pray with their bodies. We Catholics are all familiar with the various postures we employ during the Mass. We stand, we sit, we kneel, we bless ourselves with the sign of the cross, we strike our breast, we walk in procession. So why not use gestures and postures at other times to give expression to what is in our hearts?

For instance, we can simply pay attention to our breathing. Our breath is a wonderful sign of the life we have been given by

God. As we breathe in, we can imagine ourselves drawing in the very life of God; and as we exhale, we can think of breathing as letting go of whatever negative energy might be blocking God's loving presence within us.

Or we may extend our hands in a gesture of welcoming God's gifts to us this day. The same gesture can express our willingness to give our time, energy and service to whatever God is asking of us. We might turn to the four directions with our arms outstretched in a gesture of praise and thanksgiving for all that God has created.

We might engage in a "sacred walk" wherein we simply walk in silent wonder at the goodness of life all around us. One popular form of sacred walk nowadays is the labyrinth—a circular path that is walked in silence, simply trusting that the path will lead us to the center, the symbol of where God dwells.

We Catholics also have a tradition of kneeling in humble adoration before the Blessed Sacrament in silent gratitude for the presence of Jesus in the Eucharist and in our everyday lives. We may even be moved to "dance before the Lord" as King David did when the ark of the covenant was carried into Jerusalem (see 2 Samuel 6:14). A friend of mine told me recently that during her retreat she danced alone in the snow on a beautiful moonlit night. It was a profound spiritual experience for her.

### Contemplation and Action

One final point I want to make about contemplative prayer is that there is no focus on decision or action, no specific resolution to change something about ourselves or our situation. Indeed, it is sometimes seen as a weakness or criticism of contemplative prayer that it seems too inward-looking, has too much "God-and-me" emphasis with no connection to love or service of neighbor. But in actual experience, the evidence shows that those who practice contemplative prayer are often actively engaged in the world. This makes sense. When we are deeply immersed in the presence and love of God, we want to be fully in tune with the will of God—which is the healing and salvation of all in the human family.

Contemplative prayer—indeed, all genuine prayer—ought to energize us for service and compassion. The Zen masters say that after we have achieved enlightenment through meditation we are to return to the marketplace to save all living things. Saint Teresa of Ávila, a great contemplative, was a dynamo of action. "We should desire and engage in prayer," she said, "not for our enjoyment, but for the sake of gaining the strength which fits us for service."

But the other side of the equation is equally true: We will not be able to serve our neighbor or remain faithful to God unless we are deeply grounded in prayer. As another of my Capuchin brothers, Ellis Zimmer, has said so well, "Ministry without some inner fire accompanying one's words or deeds is a pallid substitute for Christian service, a wooden exercise, a gift bereft of soul."

Let us not separate what belongs together: prayer and action, mind and heart, love of God and love of neighbor.

### Questions for Reflection or Discussion

1. Have you ever attempted formal meditation or contemplation? Describe what happened.

2. What does it mean to say that prayer can be "dangerous"? Tell a story of when prayer has led you to do something you otherwise would not have done.

3. Give an example of something that was "more than meets the eye." What was it that caught your attention? How did you come to realize its significance?

4. If you were going to take one word or phrase to pray over, what would it be? Why?

5. Describe one time when you actually "prayed with your body." How did you feel afterwards?

## Prayer Activity

Do the guided meditation of going to your favorite place as described on pages 54-55.

## Chapter Six

# Prayer for Healing

Praying for healing may sound foreign to some of us Catholics. Over the years we may have absorbed the idea that suffering, whether physical or emotional, should be borne with patience and resignation rather than relieved. "Offer it up!" was the advice we were given. Indeed, there is such a thing as redemptive suffering, as we shall see later. But as we are coming to see more clearly, there is another truth we need to keep in focus. Ordinarily, God's desire is for our wholeness and health, not for sickness and suffering.

Scripture is a powerful witness to this truth. I once read that about one fifth of the gospels are stories of healing. That tells us a great deal about how Jesus saw his mission. In calling himself the Good Shepherd, he contrasted himself with those who parade as spiritual leaders but are really thieves and destroyers of the sheep. "I came," Jesus said, "that they may have life, and have it abundantly" (John 10:10). "Life in abundance" is what Jesus came to bring us. That is why we see him involved in such an extensive healing ministry.

Moreover, it is clear that Jesus wanted the ministry of healing to be continued in the church. We note how he linked together the two gifts, preaching and healing, when he first sent the disciples out on mission: "As you go, proclaim the good news: 'The kingdom of heaven has come near.' Cure the sick, raise the dead, cleanse the lepers, cast out demons" (Matthew 10:7-8). And in the Acts of the Apostles, we see the disciples continuing the healing ministry in powerful yet natural ways. We need only recall Peter and John's cure of the lame man (see Acts 3:1-10) and Paul's exorcism of the slave girl who had magical powers (see Acts 16:16-18).

Over the centuries, however, the ministry of healing in the church became limited in the minds of many to the Anointing of the Sick, and even that had been reduced to the "last rites" administered at the moment of death. In recent years, however, the sacrament has been restored to its primary purpose as a rite of healing, even for people who are not in danger of death. Moreover, we have witnessed the wonderful, rapid growth of non-sacramental forms of prayer for healing.

### The Need for Healing

Healing prayer begins with a simple basic truth: We are all in need of healing. When we gather in church for the eucharistic liturgy, we know there are stories of pain behind the faces of the people we see. Some are suffering from chronic physical ailments such as arthritis, heart disease, diabetes, cancer. Others are in various stages of grief over a loss: death of a loved one, divorce, a broken friendship, loss of a job, failure in school. Others are in troubled marriages or are worried about their children. Still others are bearing the cross of emotional illnesses such as chronic anxiety or depression. Some people are in the grip of addiction or are living with one who is addicted. And some have been wounded at some earlier stage of life and are still bearing the emotional scars. No doubt each of us can find ourselves in one or more of these categories. This is simply the human condition. "Sooner or later," as someone has said, "life will break your heart."

Our belief as Christians, however, is that God cares about our wounds and our illnesses. The story of the man born blind (see John 9:1-41) clearly shows Jesus rejecting the idea that illness or suffering is some kind of punishment for sin. When Jesus was asked by a leper to cure him, the leper said, "Lord, if you choose, you can make me clean" (Matthew 8:2). Jesus' response was immediate and emphatic: "I do choose. Be made clean!" (Matthew 8:3). Over and over in the gospels we read that Jesus was "moved with compassion" at the sight of human suffering. Biblical scholars note that the Greek expression here is unusually strong; it literally means "his intestines were stirred up." Jesus felt the pain of others viscerally. And it moved him to healing prayer and touch.

Christians believe "Jesus Christ is the same—yesterday, today, and forever" (Hebrews 13:8). What Jesus did for hurting people of his time he continues to do for us today. Our part in the healing process is to pray. This also has strong biblical roots. For example, Psalm 41 is an eloquent plea for healing, and Psalm 30 is a heartfelt prayer of thanksgiving for recovery from a serious illness: "O Lord my God, I cried to you for help, and you have healed me.... You have turned my mourning into dancing; you have taken off my sackcloth and clothed me with joy" (Psalm 30:2, 11). And James exhorts the Christians of his time: "Are any among you suffering? They should pray" (James 5:13).

### Attitudes toward Healing

We Christians need to remember, however, that prayer for healing is never a substitute for seeking medical or psychological help. God has gifted humans with both medical knowledge and a wide variety of healing resources. Therefore, our first response to physical illness or unremitting emotional distress should be to seek the aid of a physician, psychiatrist or counselor.

At the same time, we can bring our pain to God and ask for the gift of healing. Often, too, part of our healing process may be the act of sharing our burden with others and asking them for prayers. The purpose of this is not to dump our problems onto our loved ones nor to seek their advice or elicit their sympathy. But it is well-known that "a burden shared seems only half as heavy," especially when we know that others are praying with us for healing.

We also need to pray with the proper attitudes. The first of these is *faith*. So often in the gospels, when people approached Jesus for healing, he would ask them to profess faith in him. For example, he asked two blind men: "Do you believe I am able to do this?" (Matthew 9:28). Or Jesus would praise the faith they had already shown: "Daughter, your faith has made you well; go in peace, and be healed of your disease" (Mark 5:34).

When we pray for healing, we recall that God's desire is for our health and wholeness. The Risen Jesus is present to us with the very same healing power he possessed when he walked this earth. We can approach him with absolute confidence as we pray, "Lord, I believe and trust in your saving love. In your

**65**

goodness, heal me of this affliction."

Another key attitude in healing prayer is *gratefulness* for what God has already done for us. We are much more than the sum of our problems. We have been gifted and graced in so many ways. Perhaps we can even recognize some good that has come out of our illness or our suffering. Earlier I mentioned Capuchin Father Solanus Casey, who was renowned for his ministry of healing prayer. He would often ask people to "thank God ahead of time" for whatever God was going to do for them. He was profoundly convinced that God can give only good gifts in answer to our prayers, though the responses may not be exactly what we prayed for. "Thank God ahead of time" was Father Casey's way of calling people to faith in the One he always referred to as "the good God."

This leads into a third attitude required for healing prayer. We might call it *surrender*. That is, we must be receptive and open to whatever God chooses to do in response to our prayer. Henri Nouwen said that our waiting for God must be "open-ended." This means we do not demand that our prayer be answered precisely as and when we desire. Rather, we yield graciously to God's plan and timing. "God calls us to wait open-ended," Nouwen insisted, "giving up all control and placing our unconditional trust in him."

Sometimes we may have to wait a long time for healing. Jesuit Father Matthew Linn has described the long, painful journey that finally led to his healing. At age six, his younger brother died of bronchitis. Matthew blamed himself for the death but repressed the memory. For years he was tortured with self-doubt and feelings of unworthiness, despite his intellectual gifts. Finally he began to pray for healing, and gradually he was freed of the heavy burden of shame. Ever since, Father Linn and his brother Dennis have been teaching the benefits of healing prayer around the world.

### Forgiveness and Healing

The attitude of surrender includes another crucial aspect: the willingness to *forgive* those who may have hurt us. It is no secret that some of our deepest physical or psychological wounds have been inflicted, consciously or not, by other people. An obvious example is physical or sexual abuse. In recent years more and more cases of such abuse have come to light. Abused persons are truly victims. They have had their trust betrayed, their minds and bodies violated. On a less severe basis, others have suffered from defective parenting, cruel teasing by peers, or ridicule by teachers or other people in positions of authority. Many others have had their hearts broken by marital infidelity.

At first it seems unrealistic to ask people who have suffered these traumas to forgive their offenders, especially when the latter make no effort to apologize or to seek forgiveness. But on the other hand, what is the alternative? To hang on to resentment and anger, justified as it may be? In the end, that is counterproductive. For one thing, there is no effect on the offenders. They go on their merry way, usually unaware of the feelings of those they have harmed. So now the victims are paying a double penalty—the original injury plus now the negative energy of carrying around the resentment for it. This is why the need for forgiveness is being proclaimed not just by theologians and preachers but by mental health professionals. Indeed, Dr. Robert Enright at the University of Wisconsin has founded the International Forgiveness Institute, a group of theologians and psychologists who study forgiveness as a positive mental health phenomenon.

My own belief is that forgiveness involves more than psychotherapy. The latter may be necessary to uncover the painful memories we may have repressed so that we can understand how we were hurt and who our offenders were. But at some point we will need to make the decision to forgive, which is a spiritual move that may go counter to our natural tendency to hold on to our anger. This is especially likely when the offender has been a parent or a person representing the church (as in the horrendous cases of pedophilia that have come to light in the past few years).

The only way to ever come to the point where we are *able* to forgive, I believe, is to pray for the *grace* to forgive. In my practice of counseling and spiritual direction, I have seen powerful breakthroughs toward healing after people begin praying for the ability to forgive. Sometimes it takes a long time before that particular grace can be accepted, however, because we fear that if we forgive our offender we are condoning what he or she did.

In these cases, the truth is more along these lines: What was done to us was wrong, and we were powerless at the time to prevent it. But now we are at a new moment. Forgiveness is for *our* benefit. We are trying to become free of our offender's psycho-spiritual bondage over us. Even more, we are trying to be faithful to what God asks of us: "Forgive each other, just as the Lord has forgiven you" (Colossians 3:13). Sometimes when people are struggling with forgiving someone who has committed a particularly awful sin against them, I say, "If you cannot yet forgive, then start by praying for the *desire* to forgive." Because it is also God's desire that we forgive, such a prayer will, I believe, always be granted.

### An Example of Healing Prayer

We often wonder just how we can or should pray for healing. As you may have guessed, there is no single formula for it. Some books contain beautiful prayers for healing that the authors have composed or compiled. But we can also feel free to simply turn to Christ and talk to him in our own words. I like to use the image of the two disciples walking along with Jesus on the road to Emmaus (Luke 24:13-35). As you recall the story, it is the day of his resurrection, but the two disciples do not yet believe. They are still in shock and grief over his death. Jesus approaches them, but they do not recognize him. He asks them why they seem so sad, and they pour out their feelings. He listens empathically to them, but then he proceeds to lay out a whole different perspective on the events they have witnessed. It was a profoundly healing moment for them: "Were not our hearts burning within us," they exclaimed, "while he was talking to us on the road, while he was opening the scriptures to us?" (Luke 24:32).

When praying for healing, we can visualize ourselves walking along or sitting in the presence of Jesus. He invites us to share with him how our life is going. So we proceed to tell him how and why we are in need of healing. Maybe it's the first time we've ever done that. Or maybe it's the ninety-fifth time. It really doesn't matter. What matters is that we are talking about our pain and asking for help. We are communicating with our God, even it if takes the form of begging or complaining. Here is a prayer I have composed and sometimes use, either alone or when I am leading a group in healing prayer:

Lord Jesus, I praise and thank you for each and every moment of my life up to the present. Because I believe in your gracious, unconditional love for me, I have the courage to approach you now and to ask for your gift of healing.

I ask you to enter into my heart and touch all those life experiences that need to be healed. Help me to walk closely with you, Lord, so that I might accept your healing whenever and however you wish to give it. I trust that your infinite power will refashion and heal me (even though I may not immediately see it), because you know and love me even more than I know and love myself.

Walk with me, Lord, through my life and heal those memories that are painful for me. You know I have made some mistakes, Lord. I know you understand and forgive me; but help me now with the more difficult task of forgiving myself. If I have been hurt or rejected by others, help me to forgive them as you would, "for they did not know what they were doing." And grant me, through your healing love, a deeper sense of my dignity and value in your eyes.

And now, Jesus, help me to see you walking with me in this present stage of my life. Heal those places in me where I am still wounded, especially _____. Above all, remove whatever barriers in me are preventing your love from reaching me or preventing me from extending your love to others.

Lord Jesus, into your hands I entrust my body, my spirit, and my entire being. Amen.

## When Healing Does Not Happen

One of the problems with healing prayer is that it does not always seem to "work." In spite of our fervent and persistent prayers, the cancer spreads; we do lose our job; our child does get in trouble; our marriage crumbles; our loved ones die. Now what? The temptation is to conclude that our prayers were wasted, or that they were not good enough, or that God has abandoned us. We may be tempted to quit praying altogether, or at least to stop praying for healing. Somehow we know these thoughts are probably silly, but the nagging question remains: What went wrong with our prayer for healing?

As you may recall, earlier in this book I claimed that no genuine prayer ever goes unanswered, though the answer may not be in the form we were expecting. Based on the teachings of Jesus, I maintained that our good God can give only good gifts. This truth is even more operative in our prayer for healing.

My Capuchin brother, Father Dan Crosby, has helped me with this. He makes an important distinction between "being cured" and "being healed." Cure takes place when the problem has been removed, taken away. Jesus in the gospels cured people. The blind recover their sight; the lepers are cleansed of their disease; the paralyzed man walks back to his house; the woman with the hemorrhage bleeds no longer. Today, real cures often occur through the miracle of modern medicine. Whether we are seeking a spiritual or a medical miracle, "cure" is usually what we are implicitly hoping for in healing prayer.

As we well know, however, cures do not always happen, no matter how competent the medicine or fervent the prayer. Yet even people who are not "cured" are often definitely "healed." That is, the illness or condition is not removed but the person is somehow transformed. Crosby saw this happen in the case of his own brother, Pat. Eighteen years earlier, Pat had been diagnosed with esophageal cancer. Through a combination of medical treatment and the prayers of many people, Pat was cured. But two years later the cancer returned in his bladder and pancreas. Despite a vigorous fight and the support of numerous prayers, this time there was no cure. Pat died. But everyone who

**70**

knew him had witnessed a wonderful transformation. Throughout his long illness, Pat maintained a positive and cheerful attitude. He grew close to his family and friends. For many years he had paid little attention to his religion. Through the "healing" process, Pat became a deeply spiritual man and died at peace with God and with himself.

Each of us has had similar personal experiences. We may not have received the cure we prayed for, but we know we were healed. We grew in patience, in inner peace, in gentle surrender to God's will and purpose for us. We became more compassionate toward the suffering of others. We discovered a reservoir of inner resources we never knew we had. Our trust in God grew stronger. We received the grace to forgive others and ourselves and to be freed from anger and hurt that were paralyzing us. Even when we have prayed for a loved one not to die, we have somehow found ourselves being healed of our fears and discovering spiritual strength to move forward with our lives after the death. All of this leads me to conclude: No prayer for healing is ever wasted.

I believe this is what we mean when we talk about "redemptive suffering." Our first response to suffering should always be to be delivered from it. God's deepest desire is for our wholeness and health. So we seek help and pray for cure. But if our prayer is not granted, then we ask for the grace to endure and embrace our suffering so that it may transform us at a deeper spiritual level. We unite our suffering with that of Jesus and ask him to use it for his redemptive purpose: our own spiritual good or that of someone else who may need conversion or healing. This truth has deep roots in our spiritual tradition. Through the centuries it has enabled Christians to find meaning in the midst of their suffering.

I conclude this chapter with the beautiful words of the Letter to the Hebrews: "For we do not have a high priest who is unable to sympathize with our weaknesses; but we have one who in every respect has been tested as we are.... Let us therefore approach the throne of grace with boldness, so that we may receive mercy and find grace to help in time of need" (Hebrews 4:15-16).

## Questions for Reflection or Discussion

1. When have you experienced the need for healing for yourself or others? Describe the circumstances.

2. Did you pray for healing? Why or why not?

3. If you did pray for healing, how did you handle the reality that your prayers might not be answered—at least in the way you requested?

4. What is the connection in your mind between forgiveness and healing?

5. How could you better incorporate into your prayer for healing the attitudes of faith, gratefulness and surrender?

---

### Prayer Activity

Write out on a piece of paper the prayer for healing found on pages 69-70. Take the paper to a "sacred space"—a church, the woods, a body of water—and offer it to God. (If you are unable to go yourself, ask a friend to take it for you.)

---

# Chapter Seven

# **Praying with Others**

So far we have been looking at prayer as an individual, personal activity. And we were right in doing so, for that is how most of us pray. Jesus told us that we should not pray in such a way as to be noticed by others. Rather, we should "go into your room and shut the door and pray to your Father who is in secret; and your Father who sees in secret will reward you" (Matthew 6:6).

But there is another side to the coin. We are by nature social beings. At times we feel the need to pray in the company of other people. It's a lot like embarking on an exercise or diet program. If we try to do it alone, we usually don't stick with it for very long. But if we have a couple of friends to accompany us to the class or the fitness center, we are much more likely to persevere. This is part of the reason for the success of groups like Alcoholics Anonymous, Al-Anon and Gamblers Anonymous (not to mention Weight Watchers and Jenny Craig): There is a built-in system of support and accountability.

This is why, through the centuries, believers have engaged in various forms of communal prayer. The Israelites of the Old Testament believed they were a holy people, bound together with each other and with God by a solemn covenant. So they gathered regularly for communal prayer and worship. Jesus himself participated in his people's Sabbath observance (see Luke 4:16) and in their religious festivals such as Passover and the Feast of Booths. Also, from the very beginning the first Christians came together regularly for communal prayer and "the breaking of bread" (see Acts 2:42). They were mindful of what Jesus had also told the apostles: "Where two or three are gathered in my name, I am there among them" (Matthew 18:20). Indeed, something special seems to take place when people come together for common prayer. This is why Buddhist monks try to meditate in common, even though meditation is a highly individualized activity. They believe that a certain spiritual energy is generated when people are praying together in a common space.

### Forms of Communal Prayer

Many older Catholics can recall what we called "popular devotions." When I was growing up, for example, my parents would pull my siblings and me away from our Sunday evening radio programs to attend rosary devotions, litanies and Benediction of the Blessed Sacrament at our parish church. On Friday nights, we were expected to participate in a weekly holy hour that included a sermon and prayers in honor of the Sacred Heart of Jesus. Even though we five children went grumbling, we knew it was right to be there. It was during World War II, and we were praying for peace and for the safety of our loved ones. On Tuesday nights we would sometimes accompany my mother to Mother of Perpetual Help devotions. For myself, there was something beautiful and uplifting about those hours, and I believe they had a part in my desire to become a priest.

After the Second Vatican Council, most of these devotions died out. They were said to be sentimental, pietistic, based on inadequate theology, and valued only by the elderly. Furthermore, it was claimed that they tend to detract from the Eucharistic liturgy, which ought to be the center of Catholic prayer and worship.

As valid as these claims may have been, the decline of popular devotions left a void in the souls of many people. So it was not long before other forms of communal prayer began to emerge in new ways. One was "charismatic prayer." People would gather together to listen to a passage from scripture, spend some time in silence, then offer prayers of intercession for all sorts of needs. There were songs of praise and thanksgiving, sometimes "praying in tongues" and the laying on of hands to pray for healing. Such groups continue to meet all around the country and in many parts of the world.

Many people are not drawn to this particular form of prayer, but the idea of praying together in small groups has caught on. For instance, a good number of Catholics have participated in Cursillo or in the Renew or Christ Renews His Parish programs. Perhaps for the first time, many of us felt comfortable sharing our faith experiences with a group and praying out loud for our intentions. We felt the support of one another when we revealed our struggles, our anxieties, and even our doubts in matters of religion and spirituality.

Another form of communal prayer is gathering in small groups to reflect on scripture. This has been a wonderful experience for the good number of Catholics who were largely unfamiliar with the Bible. Sometimes it takes the form of study, using prepared programs. Other times it involves coming together informally to reflect on the Sunday scriptures, not so much for study as for making connections between the readings and our daily lives. We do not try to teach each other in these groups but simply share our faith in the light of God's word.

In general, there are two ways to engage in scripture sharing. One is to listen to a passage from the Bible and then connect it with our own experience ("from Word to life"). The other is to begin with our personal experience—some incident, positive or negative that made an impact on us—and then reflect on it in light of the Sunday scripture readings ("from life to Word"). In either case it is crucial not to let the sharing slip into an intellectual "head trip." What we are trying to share is our personal faith, not our fund of knowledge.

### Participating in Group Prayer

We may not find it easy at first to speak with one another about our faith or our spirituality. I often say, half-jokingly, that we Catholics have inherited a "bashfulness gene" when it comes to talking about the interior life. We have been conditioned to think of our faith as a strictly private domain that needs to be protected from the scrutiny of "outsiders." It is almost easier to talk about our sex life than our spiritual life—at least we get a lot more encouragement from the culture to do the former!

But when we take the risk of opening up a bit to share some of our inner world, some marvelous things can happen. For one thing, we discover that we are not alone in the ways we think and feel about things. As psychologist Carl Rogers used to say, "What is most personal is most general." That is, what we think is completely unique to ourselves is often the experience of many others, who also believe they are unique. What a relief to find, "Gee, I thought I was the only one who had these doubts-fears-hurts-impulses-questions. I guess they're pretty normal after all."

We find in prayer groups that we are accepted for who we are. We can relax and be ourselves. We don't have to put up any guard or false front. As the level of trust builds within the group, we find we are able to reveal more about ourselves and our faith journey. We can almost feel the presence of Christ in the group and in each member. Not only do we find we are accepted but we also feel cared for. If we ever are in trouble or need help, we know these people will be there for us. So we often say or think, "*This* is what Christian community is all about."

But what do we need to contribute in order to create this kind of caring atmosphere? The first ingredient, I would suggest, is a willingness to share, to reveal some of our inner world, especially our beliefs and values, our life of faith. This may not come easily for many of us. It will require some willingness to risk, to be vulnerable. After all, someone in the group may think less of us, challenge us, perhaps even ridicule us. They may place us in either the dreaded "liberal" or "traditional" camp. We may be labeled "the enemy" or dismissed as irrelevant. The only way to punch through these fears is to actually risk speaking out. If we do, we will find the group members ready to accept us as fellow seekers even though they may disagree with some of our specific perceptions. This is how the trust is built. (Speaking of trust, it is crucial that there be a "covenant of confidentiality" in these prayer groups. This means a serious agreement that nothing shared in the group will be carried to persons outside the group. We will hold in sacred trust whatever has been revealed.)

Another essential attitude to successful group prayer is our willingness to accept the sharing of others in the group. This will require us to suspend judgment, to refrain from criticism or attack. More positively, it calls us to develop a deep respect for the worth and dignity of each person in the group. We may certainly express our disagreement with a viewpoint, but always in a manner that protects the other's self-esteem. We ask questions for clarification and to aid our own understanding, but we do not engage in argumentation. And we give each person the courtesy of our full attention while they are speaking.

We always need to keep in the forefront of our minds the purpose of our gathering: to deepen prayer life. This excludes, for example, any sort of effort to "take over" the group. Sometimes a person who has a good deal of biblical knowledge (or simply has a need or propensity to teach) may bring to the group all the latest research and scholarship on the passage under discussion, while the others sit in awe while he or she expounds. (Before long, of course, the awe turns to boredom or resentment.) Certainly, there may need to be some focus on the meaning of the text in its context. But the main focus always is on what a particular passage is saying to us, on how it is calling us to deepen or change.

Finally, such sessions should always conclude with some kind of shared prayer. This may take the form of a prepared handout recited by everyone in the group, or members may be invited to offer their own spontaneous prayer—of thanksgiving, praise, intercession, healing, or whatever seems needed or appropriate.

It is not difficult to see that these kinds of prayer groups will need some sort of leadership, at least in the beginning. Otherwise, there is danger of the group floundering or going off the track, some members dominating and others withdrawing, factions developing. A skilled leader will work to facilitate the group's purpose and will model good leadership behavior for the others to continue when he or she moves on.

### Prayer Support Groups

For some time now, I have been encouraging parishes to develop prayer support groups for persons with various needs. For instance, one day or evening each month might be available for people living with cancer or other chronic illness, another for those who have lost a loved one in death, another for caregivers of handicapped children or elderly parents, another for those who are separated or divorced, and yet another for those who have lost jobs. This ministry is one that could easily lend itself to collaboration among several parishes, and these sessions need not be led by a staff member. The leadership could easily rotate among a number of laypeople.

Note that these are meant to be prayer services, not therapy groups or substitutes for therapy. Any number of formats could be imagined. Here is a possible one: gathering song; word of welcome by the leader; opening prayer; reading from the Bible; invitation to participants to share their reflections on the scripture passage and/or some of their personal story; invitation to pray aloud or silently for one's own or others' needs; recitation of a psalm or some other prayer in common; closing song and sign of peace.

These prayer groups could be a new form of "popular devotions" that would be meeting the needs of a significant number of people, including some who may not now be coming to church on a regular basis. Wherever I go, I find people wanting a deeper sense of community in a church that often seems impersonal and distant to them. We all want to experience prayer in a more personal and intimate way. We want to know we are not alone in our pain and suffering but are linked with others who are bearing similar burdens. We want to know that the compassion and healing power of Jesus are available to us, just as they were to the people of New Testament times.

Prayer in the Catholic tradition has always been a many-splendored thing: silent and vocal, individual and communal, bodily and mental, intellectual and emotional. Now, in our final chapter, we will turn our attention to what is perhaps the most familiar prayer for Catholics: the Mass.

## Questions for Reflection or Discussion

1. Have you ever been part of a discussion or support group? If so, describe your experience. What were the positives and negatives?

2. What forms of communal prayer appeal to you? Why?

3. Are you shy or reticent about praying in a group? What is holding you back? How might you overcome your hesitancy?

4. If you were to participate in a prayer support group, what kind of people would you like to have in the group— friends, strangers, people your own age, those in similar occupations or life situations? How might you find (or even organize) such a group? Who might help you?

5. In your mind, what is the difference between a prayer service and a therapy group? How could you help to keep a group focused on prayer?

## Prayer Activity

Invite four close friends to your home for a one-time prayer group. Make it for a specific occasion or intention (someone who needs your prayers or to celebrate a specific anniversary or a holy day in the church calendar, for example). If you don't feel comfortable leading the prayer group yourself, ask one of the other participants or someone from your parish staff to do so. Plan about a half hour of Bible reflection, traditional or formal prayers, spontaneous prayer and silent prayer. At the end, provide some refreshments and have some conversation. Do not schedule another session until you have had time to reflect on how you felt about the experience and have received informal feedback from your friends. Then if you want to participate in more communal prayer, either help organize your own group or join an existing prayer group in the parish.

## Chapter Eight

# The Mass as Prayer

When I was a boy attending daily Mass at our parish school, I used a little booklet titled *The Greatest Prayer: The Mass*. Complete with pictures, it accompanied me through the various parts of the Mass with short prayers I could say while the action was taking place at the altar. Today I wonder how many Catholics think of the Mass as prayer—much less the "greatest" prayer.

A few years ago I read a book on evangelization by Paulist Father Frank DeSiano entitled *Sowing New Seed*. In one of the chapters he talks about the fact that so many Catholic people, especially the younger ones, have stopped attending the Sunday liturgy. The usual reason given is that they find the Mass boring. This is in spite of all the attempts the church has made to improve the liturgical celebration: The priest now faces the people; the Mass is celebrated in our own language; there is much more variety in the scripture readings and in the music.

Yet our people are still bored. They are used to television and sports events and live concerts and stand-up comedians. So some churches try to have dramatic preaching and bigger choirs and multi-instrument accompaniment. But, says DeSiano, that is not the answer. Most priests can never measure up to Billy Graham or Martin Luther King, Jr. And no matter how great our choirs, they can't compete with MTV or the Mormon Tabernacle Choir.

No, DeSiano says, the problem lies deeper. Our people don't really come to Mass to be entertained. They can find that anywhere. The real problem is not that people are bored. It is that they are *disappointed*. Why? Because in the Mass they do not experience contact with God. They do not feel touched by God. And that is what they are hoping for when they come to worship. They know instinctively that Mass is prayer. And they are disappointed because too often they experience the Mass not as heartfelt prayer but as merely going through the motions without heart or soul.

Father Eugene Walsh talked about this in his book *The Ministry of the Celebrating Community*. The purpose of Eucharistic liturgy, he said, is to create for everyone present the possibility of an experience of God, to "taste and see that the Lord is good" (Psalm 34:8). He insisted that this is possible for the average Christian for two reasons. First, the experience of God is the natural and rightful destiny of every one of us who are baptized, not just for a few "chosen souls." We are *made* for relationship with God. And second, God is always reaching out to us in love, inviting us into personal relationship. Therefore, Walsh says, the purpose of the Mass is to recognize and celebrate the presence of God giving hope and meaning to our lives. How can this, then, ever be boring?

What's the obstacle? What prevents this "divine connection" from happening? Walsh would say that it is the apathy and passivity of the congregation, but he does not lay the blame on them. "We have brought it on ourselves," he says, speaking to his fellow church leaders. We have created a gap, a gulf, between "the ministers" and "the congregation." The former are perceived as "doers" of liturgy, while the latter are relegated to "that part of the worshipping community that watches, is read to, and talked at." They are the "receivers," we ministers are the "givers." Naturally the people come to Mass in a basically passive frame of mind. They expect something to be done *to* them and *for* them instead of having the sense that they are *participants* in a vital, integral task—the ministry of the celebrating community.

### Praying the Mass

So how do we reduce the gap between ministers and congregation? How do we create a sense that "we are all in this together"? Obviously there has to be some differentiation of roles. We need a presider, readers, altar servers, ushers, music ministers, choir, eucharistic ministers. But what will connect all of these into one unified act of worship? It is nothing less than the interior conviction that we are gathered *in prayer.* We are present, both as individuals and as a believing community, in order to worship God in union with Jesus Christ and the whole "communion of saints." And we fully expect that this act of worship will open us to an experience of "contact with God" and nourish our relationship with God—which is, after all, the very definition of prayer.

Let me digress here for just a moment. Nowadays we often hear people say things like, "Why do I need to go to Mass anyway? I can experience God while praying at home or walking in the woods or on the beach." That is certainly a valid point, and I have no doubt that people do experience God in these ways, as do I.

But I believe the point that's overlooked is this: What are we missing by not praying with a community? For one thing, we are missing mutual support. As we said in the previous chapter, it is much harder to stick with a discipline, such as an exercise or diet program, all by ourselves. It is no different with the prayer of worship. If left entirely to ourselves, we can too easily find reasons and excuses to skip it.

Moreover, another important question needs to be asked: How does *God* want to be honored and worshipped? After all, our prayer life is not a unilateral activity. The key category is *relationship*, which must include at least two persons. Should we not be asking, "What sort of prayer or worship does God desire of us?" From earliest biblical times the people of God were instructed to remember and keep holy the Lord's Day. The Sabbath, as it was called, was not to be just an ordinary day. It was to be a day of rest from work, but even more it was to be a day to gather as a community in order to remember who God is and who we are, to strengthen our relationship with God by prayer, song and listening to the Word of God.

I find it very instructive that Jesus himself made it a point to join his community regularly for the sabbath service. We read in the gospel, "When he came to Nazareth, where he had been brought up, he went to the synagogue on the sabbath day, *as was his custom*" (Luke 4:16). Now it seems to me that Jesus could easily have exempted himself from this practice on the grounds that he already had a special relationship with his

Father. But he didn't. He wanted to be there with his people, praying with them, listening to scripture, coming to understand and share his people's fears, hopes and longings. I always think that if regular worship in community was good enough for Jesus, it should certainly be important to us.

In the Christian era, the Jewish practice of the Sabbath took the form of coming together each Sunday (the new "Lord's Day," based on the fact of Jesus' resurrection on Sunday) to celebrate God's wonderful deeds in human history, especially the death and resurrection of Jesus. Early Christians willingly participated in the Sunday Eucharistic liturgy (eventually called "The Mass" from the Latin words for the dismissal, *Missa Est,* "it is sent"), not so much out of obligation or fear of mortal sin but from a sense of their own need. Surrounded by a pagan society, they needed to know that they were not alone in their struggle to remain faithful to Christ and his gospel. They wanted to feel connected to their brothers and sisters in the faith. They wanted to have their minds instructed and inspired through listening to scripture. Above all, they wanted to be nourished by sharing in the very body and blood of Christ through the sacrament of Holy Communion. Then, after the power of that experience of "contact with God," they returned to their everyday world to sanctify all their activities and infuse them with love and joy. The Sunday Mass was truly prayer *par excellence.*

### Participating in the Mass

Back to our question: How do we participate in the Mass to make it a form of prayer, of connection with God, of response to God's loving initiative of relationship? In the first place, we need to come with a sense of *expectation.* That is, we anticipate, we expect, we trust that in the sacred action of the Mass we will experience God. From everyday life we know if we go out on a date or to a party or meeting convinced nothing interesting or important is going to happen that nothing will. It is the same with Mass. If we come merely out of routine or obligation, with no expectation of encountering the living God, that low expectation will be met. On the other hand, if we come with longing, with desire to be touched by God's word and filled with the joy of Christ's holy presence, that's what we are likely to find. Before the Mass begins, then, it would be good to offer a brief prayer such as, "Lord God, thank you for inviting me into this sacred event. I come to you as I am, with all my needs and burdens and imperfections. Please fill me today with your peace and love and with whatever special gift you know I need at this time."

Second, if the Mass is going to be prayerful, we will have to practice the discipline of *paying attention.* This is not easy for us as Americans because all week long there is so much that distracts us. Even at Mass, we can be put off by the people around us: the reader with his nasal voice, the cantor with her shrill tone, the priest with his annoying habits. It is difficult to "Be still and know that I am God" (Psalm 46:10). But that is just what the Mass invites us to do.

So during the entrance song we need to participate, to notice how the words and even the music speaks to our own concerns. Even when they don't touch us directly on any given day, we need to recognize that they surely relate to some of the people in the congregation and ask God to touch them with the grace they need. This is one of the many reasons why we need to take seriously our responsibility to sing with the rest of the congregation, whether we have a "nice" voice or are in the mood or not. Singing at Mass is part of the communal nature of the prayer. As Saint Augustine said, "When we sing, we pray twice."

Likewise, we must enter into the opening rites of the Mass if we are to reap its total benefit as a form of prayer. The penitential rites, where we admit our shortcomings and ask for and receive forgiveness from both God and each other, is a wonderful prayer in and of itself—almost a mini-sacrament of Reconciliation. The Kyrie, Gloria and opening prayers are also meant to get us into a prayerful frame of mind.

Next we should try to listen deeply to the scripture readings. What are they saying to us? How is it "good news"? What are the implications for our daily life? One of the best preparations for making the Mass a prayer is to preview the scripture readings, either at home or before the service begins. This can actually be a form of praying with the Bible described in chapter four, plus it has the added benefit of focusing our attention on the readings at Mass.

### Getting More Out of the Homily

Familiarity with the scripture readings for the day will also help us get more out of the homily from a prayer point of view. Sometimes the priest's reflections may closely parallel our own; other times they will take off in a totally different direction. Can we still pay attention? Perhaps there is one grain of truth we need to hear. I will never forget what my own brother Larry told me one time: "When I come to Mass on Sunday, I need to hear something that will help me spiritually to get through the week."

Speaking of the homily, let me share another digression. There is a tendency nowadays to judge the quality of the Sunday Mass solely by the preaching. If the homily was insightful, practical, humorous—and brief—the Mass was good. If not, the Mass was a dud. Now, I am all in favor of good, interesting, Bible-inspired preaching that truly connects with people's everyday lives. And—like you—I have heard my share of the opposite. I grieve for people who seldom if ever experience a good homily. They are being cheated.

But having said that, I believe we have to move to a deeper level of faith. The spiritual efficacy of the Mass does *not* depend on the homily. If we truly believe that the Mass is essentially a prayer (or better, a prayer-in-action), then its power flows from the Risen Lord Jesus. The church has always taught that the principal celebrant of every Mass is Christ himself. And insofar as our minds and hearts are united with him, the Mass achieves its purpose: reconciliation and union with God, an increase of spiritual life in Christ. An insipid homily, trite hymns, the priest's sloppy manner of praying can all detract from that sacred purpose; but they cannot invalidate it. In the end, whether or not we experience "contact with God" during the Mass depends mostly on us—on our level of participation and our openness to the grace being offered.

## Our Profession of Faith, Prayers and Offerings

The Creed can also be a difficult prayer moment for us, simply because we've said it so often. What helps me is to imagine someone asking me, "OK, what do you really believe? What gives you direction for your life? What helps you stay focused, make sense out of life's craziness?" And I answer, "I believe in one God...and the life of the world to come" (and everything else in between). The Creed is like our personal and communal "mission statement." It tells us and everyone else what we believe life is all about. Did you ever think how many people are without this? Their heads are constantly turning this way and that, wondering what "voices" (pop stars, sports heroes, talk-show celebrities) they should listen to. The Creed is our life compass.

Next comes the Prayer of the Faithful ("General Intercessions"). We want to pay attention to these also, because they are prayers that stretch us beyond ourselves. As a praying community we ask God's blessing upon our church leaders, families, religious educators, government authorities, people who are troubled and needy. We pray for an end to hunger and violence, for reverence for human life, for justice for all God's children, and for world peace. It's as if the community stretches out its arms to embrace the whole world in prayer.

During the preparation of the gifts (Offertory) we offer ourselves, together with Christ, as a gift to God. To me that means I offer my talents, my time, my energies, my work, my efforts to love and care for others—everything I am and have—for the glory of God and the service of God's people. It's a reminder of my very reason for living. And the wonderful part is that this includes even my mistakes and failures. Even they can be transformed by the power of Christ's death and resurrection into something holy.

## The Eucharistic Prayer

We come now to the very heart of the Mass: the Eucharistic Prayer. Unfortunately, this is the part that people are usually thinking of when they complain that the Mass is boring. The Eucharistic Prayer is highly structured and stylized. It is prayed by the priest alone, and it does not vary a great deal from one Mass to another. So it's not easy for people to experience themselves as active participants in this part of the Mass.

Still, we need to ask what *we* can do to involve ourselves in the Eucharistic Prayer. The answer, once again, is the simple act of "paying attention." Recall that the Eucharistic Prayer always begins with a "Preface" that has a brief dialogue between the priest and ourselves: "The Lord be with you." "And also with you." The priest invites us to "lift up our hearts" and to "give thanks to the Lord our God." And we respond, "Yes, we want to do that; that's why we're here." The Preface itself (and there are nearly ninety different ones) is always a prayer of praise and thanksgiving for all that God has done for us: the goodness of creation; the coming of Christ into our world; his suffering, dying, and rising from the dead; his sending of the Holy Spirit; his continuing work of sanctifying the world. Sometimes this theme of thanks and praise continues in the first part of the Eucharistic Prayer. If we are truly paying attention, we will often be touched by some of the beautiful expressions: "We come to you, Father, with praise and thanksgiving, through Jesus Christ your Son"; "You so loved the world that in the fullness of time you sent your only Son to be our Savior"; "for our sake he opened his arms on the cross; he put an end to death and revealed the resurrection"; "God of love and mercy, you are always ready to forgive; we are sinners, (but) you invite us to trust in your mercy." At the end of the Preface we join together in singing the "Holy, Holy" and we unite our prayer of praise and thanks with that of the angels and saints who are forever praising God in heaven (see Revelation 5:11-14).

Next the priest calls upon the power of the Holy Spirit to transform our gifts of bread and wine into the very body and blood of Jesus Christ. Then the priest recalls for us the action of Jesus at the Last Supper: how he took bread and wine, blessed it and shared it with the disciples, saying: "Take this, all of you; eat and drink. For this is my body, broken for you; this is my blood, poured out for you. Do this is remembrance of me." We surely want to pay attention during this most sacred moment.

But we need to remember that the Eucharistic Prayer is one

unified prayer and action. Every part is important, and we want to keep our attention focused. The next part is a prayer of remembering. We recall Christ's passion, death and resurrection, and we join ourselves to his great act of loving sacrifice: "We recall Christ's death, his descent among the dead, his resurrection, and his ascension to your right hand; and looking forward to his coming in glory, we offer you his body and blood, the acceptable sacrifice which brings salvation to the whole world." If we are paying attention, we will want to consciously unite ourselves to this action of Jesus. We offer to God all that we have and are, so that we can participate with Christ and with one another in the redemption of the world.

Next we turn our minds to the needs of God's people everywhere. We pray for the members of the church, leaders and faithful; we remember those who have died; and we include all those who are seeking God "with a sincere heart." This always makes me think of our young people who no longer attend our churches, as well as those who are struggling to find some kind of spiritual direction for their troubled lives. We conclude with a prayer for ourselves and our final salvation: "We hope to enjoy forever the vision of your glory." Finally, the priest proclaims the great Doxology: "Through him (Christ), with him, and in him, in the unity of the Holy Spirit, all glory and honor is yours, almighty Father, forever and ever." And we pray or sing our wholehearted "Amen."

The Eucharistic Prayer lasts only for a few moments. But it is a powerful, majestic prayer. I am convinced that if we truly listen, if we let those words come into our minds and hearts, our spirits will be lifted up and nourished.

### Communion and Dismissal

If we pay attention to the Eucharistic Prayer, we will be well-disposed to a unique moment of human contact with both God and one another. This is the part of the Mass where we actually receive the living body and blood of Christ in Holy Communion. After first admitting that we are not worthy to do so but that God can heal our soul with a word, we proclaim once again that this is the "Lamb of God, who takes away the sins of the world" and ask for his mercy. Then together as a congregation we file up to receive Jesus, singing as we do. Then there is a few moments of silence, when we can briefly practice the kind of meditation and contemplation described in chapter five.

And, finally, after closing prayers and a final blessing, we are ready to leave Mass, having been spiritually enriched by perhaps the best form of prayer we Catholics have. Perhaps my little book, *The Greatest Prayer: The Mass,* was right on target.

Speaking of leaving, let me say a word about the rite of dismissal. Unfortunately, the words the priest uses at the end of Mass do not really express the church's intention. "The Mass is ended, go in peace," or "Go, the Mass is ended," seem to imply, "Well, now that's over with; we can get on with business-as-usual." But the real point of that dismissal is a *sending forth.* The priest is sending us out on mission. It's as if he is saying: "What we have done here is not finished. We are to go forth and *live* what we have celebrated here. Jesus Christ has come to us in the Mass with his saving love. He has blessed us, forgiven us, healed us. But he has also empowered us—to go forth and bring his blessing and healing into our part of the world, to the people we live with and work with and mingle with socially. What we have listened to in scripture and in the prayers, the spiritual food and drink we have received—let's not keep it to ourselves. Let's go forth and share it with people everywhere."

## Questions for Reflection or Discussion

1. Estimate how many times you have participated in Mass in your lifetime. What percentage of the time have you consciously thought of the Mass as a prayer? How do you feel about that percentage?

2. How can you better experience contact with God at Mass? What could you do to better prepare yourself or put yourself in a more active frame of mind?

3. Which parts of the Mass do you find the most prayerful and fulfilling? To which parts do you find it most difficult to pay attention? Why?

4. Give three good reasons for going to Mass. Give at least one good reason not to go. Which reasons are more compelling, and why?

5. What does the practice of Sabbath or "keeping holy the Lord's Day" mean to you? How does going to Mass fit into that practice?

---

### Prayer Activity

Go to Mass at a different church from the one that you are used to attending. Try to imagine that you are going to Mass for the very first time ever. Allow yourself to be surprised and aware of each element of the Mass. Let yourself respond with your heart, not your head, to what is being said and done. Give yourself permission to become emotionally involved in the liturgy. Feel the presence of God. Stay at least five minutes after the Mass has ended and reflect on the Mass as a prayer. If you want, write your reflections down when you return home. Read those reflections or recall the experience before you attend Mass the next time in your own parish.

# Conclusion

My hope in writing this book is that it would serve as an invitation to readers to actually pray—better, more often, with more fervor, and with greater fulfillment. Whether you are just beginning to pray, have done so all your life, desire to go deeper or are searching for alternative ways to pray—I hope the book will be an aid. As we have seen, our Catholic community has a long tradition and a rich treasury of prayer on which we can draw.

Finally, a word of encouragement to those who are experiencing some kind of block, or for whom prayer has become dry and seemingly unfruitful. Please do not stop trying to pray. The very act of setting aside a certain part of your day or night for prayer—even if you are fatigued or distracted the whole time—is a prayer. You are giving God that most precious gift: your time. Even if you are not praying, at least your body is praying. It is saying, "I want to be here, in the presence of God, and nowhere else." Your very desire and your bodily presence are prayers that are not in vain.

We can all draw encouragement from these beautiful words of Saint Paul: "Likewise the Spirit helps us in our weakness; for we do not know how to pray as we ought, but that very Spirit intercedes with sighs too deep for words. And God, who searches the heart, knows what is the mind of the Spirit, because the Spirit intercedes for the saints according to the will of God" (Romans 8:26-27).

How comforting to know that when prayer seems impossible for us, the Holy Spirit takes over, prays on our behalf, puts into divine language what our poor hearts cannot express. When our words fail us, our God does not.

## Additional Catholic Resources

**INVITATION TO CATHOLICISM**
**Beliefs + Teachings + Practices**
ALICE CAMILLE
Everyone from lifelong Catholics to interested non-Catholics will welcome the easy-to-understand, logical explanations found in this overview of Catholic beliefs and Church teachings. Discussion questions, activities and an appendix containing the words to many prayers make it ideal for adults joining the Church, those returning to the active practice of their faith, and people who want to move beyond what they learned as children in religion class.
240 pages, paperback, $9.95

**JESUS AND HIS MESSAGE**
**An Introduction to the Good News**
REV. LEO MAHON
A clear, concise introduction to who Jesus was and what he taught, focusing on his ministry of teaching and healing, his passion, death and resurrection. The practical, down-to-earth format with reflections / discussion questions makes this book perfect for individuals or groups.
112 pages, paperback, $6.95

**LIFE IN CHRIST**
**A Catholic Catechism for Adults**
REVS. GERARD WEBER and JAMES KILLGALLON
Over 2 million copies sold! Written in the traditional question-and-answer format, it is the #1 adult Catholic catechism. Extensively revised in accordance with the *Catechism of the Catholic Church,* it contains hundreds of scriptural references and quotations. A great family reference book with a helpful index.
336 pages, paperback, $6.95

**Available from booksellers or call 800-397-2282**